Tracing Your
Civil War Ancestor

Tracing Your
Civil War Ancestor

BERTRAM HAWTHORNE GROENE

JOHN F. BLAIR, *Publisher*
Winston-Salem, North Carolina

Fourth Edition,
Fourth Printing, 2004

The paper in this book meets the guidelines
for permanence and durability of the
Committee on Production Guidelines
for Book Longevity of the Council
on Library Resources.

Library of Congress Cataloging-in-Publication Data
Groene, Bertram Hawthorne, 1924–
    Tracing your Civil War ancestor / Bertram Hawthorne Groene. — 4th ed.
        p.   cm.
    Includes bibliographical references and index.
    ISBN 0-89587-123-8
    1. United States—History—Civil War, 1861–1865—Archival resources—
Directories.   2. United States—Genealogy—Handbooks, manuals, etc.   I. Title.
CD3047.G76   1995
929'.1'072073—dc20   94-47605

For My Parents

Charles Bertram and Lucille Hawthorne Groene

Contents

Illustrations

\

Acknowledgments

In creating a guidebook such as this, an author very soon finds himself indebted to many people. I will list here only a few: Mr. Richard Frisbie, publisher and owner of Hope Farm Press and Bookshop; Michael Musick, military historian and archivist of the Old Army Branch of the National Archives; John Peterson, National Park Service project manager; Robert Reilly, author and expert on United States military weapons; Bob Younger of Morningside Press, a nationally known authority on and publisher of Civil War books; Tom Broadfoot, a tireless reprinter of outstanding Civil War books and indexes; Dr. J. Larry Crain, martial arms expert; and H. E. Howard of H. E. Howard, Inc., publisher of many Civil War books. All of these persons were a source of aid and comfort by giving help, advice, and encouragement.

The author also wishes to express his appreciation to the following publishers and others who graciously gave their consent for the use of illustrative material and helped in various ways:

To the Louisiana State University Press for permission to reproduce a page from *Civil War Books,* by Allan Nevins, James I. Robertson, Jr., and Bell I. Wiley.

To the New York Public Library for permission to reproduce two pages from Volume II of *Military Bibliography of the Civil War*, by Charles E. Dornbusch.

To A. S. Barnes & Company, Inc., for permission to reproduce a page from its edition of *A Compendium of the War of the Rebellion*, by Frederick H. Dyer.

To the University of Illinois Press for permission to reproduce a page from its edition of *Historical Register and Dictionary of the United States Army*, by Francis B. Heitman.

To the Yale University Press for permission to reproduce a page from *A Guide to Archives and Manuscripts in the United States*, edited by Philip M. Hamer.

To Robert M. Reilly for permission to reproduce a page from his book, *United States Military Small Arms, 1816–1865*, published by The Eagle Press, Inc., Baton Rouge, Louisiana, and also for permission to raid his bibliography for material for my Appendix C.

To the Library of Congress for invaluable assistance.

To the National Archives for permission to reproduce a number of records.

Last, I am indebted to my wife Peggy, who typed, edited, and helped revise this book many times since its inception.

Introduction

This book has ben especially designed as a guide for those who are descendants of Civil War veterans. It should also be highly useful to collectors of Civil War equipment and to antique dealers.

Descendants of Civil War veterans can use this book to help trace the military careers of their forebears, to follow their battles and camp experiences, and to study in depth the histories of their military and naval units. With luck, the book may even lead to a photograph of great-grandfather or his comrades and officers.

Collectors of Civil War items can use this guide to trace names inscribed on weapons and other military equipment, thus regaining for such items a lost time and place in history.

Antique dealers should find the book useful in that it not only aids in establishing a history for inscribed photographs, weapons, and other items, but directs them to the most authoritative sources when they are searching for the identification of Civil War equipment. With its help, they should be able to answer such questions as "Is this truly of the Civil War period?" and even "What is it?"

*Tracing Your
Civil War Ancestor*

Scabbard of the sword carried by the officer who stopped the Confederate
fleet in the last fight between ironclads in the Civil War.
A complete inscription such as this makes a search much easier.

The Value
of a Search

ON THE TABLE IN FRONT OF ME as I write lies a Civil War officer's
sword. It has a bright brass guard, and the handle is wrapped, as they
were in those days, with sharkskin bound with neatly twisted brass wire.
Inscribed on the brass top of the metal scabbard is

Presented to
LT. E. P. MASON
1st Conn Artillery
by his friends in
New Haven

On May 11, 1861, one month after the Civil War began, strapping,
nineteen-year-old, six-foot Ebenezer Mason of Litchfield, Connecticut,
walked into a Hartford recruiting station. Here he enlisted as a private in
the Fourth Connecticut Infantry. Seven months later the Fourth Connecticut was changed to the First Connecticut Heavy Artillery, and now
Mason found himself an artillery corporal. In the following months

Mason and his comrades hauled their huge mortars and giant rifled cannon into battle after battle as the Union army under McClellan pressed on toward the Rebel capital of Richmond.

In December 1862, Ebenezer was promoted to second lieutenant and was in the bloody tragedies of Fredericksburg, Chancellorsville, and Gettysburg. Mason lived through these battles to become a first lieutenant commanding his own fort, Battery Sawyer, perched on the high south bank of the James River some twelve miles southeast of the Confederate capital. This was an important position, for it protected a water barrier of boats, nets, and masts which the Union army had thrown up across the river. This barrier had been built to prevent a large Confederate fleet trapped up the James River near Richmond from suddenly steaming down the river, anchoring off City Point, Grant's supply base, and shelling that huge depot to a smoking ruin.

On the night of January 23, 1865, an eleven-ship fleet headed by three giant Confederate ironclads, *Fredericksburg, Richmond,* and *Virginia,* attempted just that. Lieutenant Mason's two huge seacoast mortars, which could toss hundred-pound balls a mile in the air, and one large cannon, which could throw a hundred-pound shell over two thousand yards, went into action. They filled the dark, winding river below them with thousands upon thousands of pounds of shells, grapeshot, and canister. Up the river from City Point came the Federal ironclad, *Conestoga,* and because of its fire, that of two other small forts, and Lieutenant Mason's constant battering, the ships of the Confederate fleet were forced to turn their prows west and steam, crippled and defeated, back up the river toward the capital. So ended the last battle with ironclads in the Civil War. Mason's bravery and cool judgment under fire earned him the two bars of a captain of artillery.

Two months later the fatigue, exposure, and strain of more than three years of constant battle took their final toll, and Captain Mason—whether violently or quietly we shall never know—slipped into insanity and was discharged from the army. Throughout the rest of his life Ebenezer Mason was in and out of mental institutions, finally dying childless, divorced, and bitter, in 1911, at the age of sixty-nine.

Captain Mason's story was not a difficult one to trace, and you should

be able to do the same with your own soldier's story, with a little time and at very little expense, by following the suggestions in this book.

The ever-growing number of descendants of Johnny Reb and Billy Yank can be divided into several categories. There are those who honestly admit that they know little or absolutely nothing about great-grandfather's war experiences. Most descendants fall into this category. There are those, innocent and pure of heart, who have had handed down to them, intact and without benefit of research, a complete history. A hundred years of time, the faded memories of the old folk, and a few tall tales thrown in that grow more grand with each retelling take their toll. What finally emerges as great-grandfather's history may well resemble the script of a Hollywood historical extravaganza and contain just about as much truth. Then there are those few who really have a complete account of their ancestor passed to them through letters and diaries, but here and there great-grandfather may have stretched a point or two for the "folks back home."

In any case, after reading this book, perhaps you will be one of those brave few who will "go a-searching" on the trail of your forebears and will place your trust in the records whenever you can. You will have tried to find the truth about a noble ancestor. What better tribute could one pay to those who fought in that far-off war than to retrace their steps, buried and forgotten for three generations?

The knowledge of historical research that this book gives will, I hope, provide a history to those who have none, correct fanciful and erroneous histories and replace them with fact, and finally, give additional details to incomplete lives already partially researched by proud and concerned descendants.

Unknown to most people, there are millions of impersonal state and federal records and thousands of books that have preserved literally hundreds of thousands of soldiers' lives and wartime experiences. To those with the know-how of Civil War research they will open the door and unlock the past. An identifying name and regiment can lift any long-dead soldier's personal equipment out of the great flood of existing guns, swords, knives, boots, spurs, or whatever and give it a distinct identity, a place in time, and above all, an authentic history.

mortars on Cemetery Hill battery, which was firing on our troops in rear
of Fort Haskell. The other mortars were directed on the batteries
near the Petersburg pike. They burst a large number of shell in the
fort, wounding four men of the Fifty-first Pennsylvania; no casualties
in Company A. They opened one new mortar where they were digging
day before yesterday, in rear of the Crater.

Very respectfully, your obedient servant,

H. D. PATTERSON,
Lieutenant, First Connecticut Artillery, Commanding Battery.

Lieut. W. S. MALONY,
Acting Assistant Adjutant-General, Siege Batteries.

No. 16.

*Report of Lieut. Ebenezer P. Mason, First Connecticut Heavy Artillery,
commanding Battery Sawyer, of operations January 23–24.*

BATTERY SAWYER,
James River, Va., January 29, 1865.

SIR: Pursuant to instructions from headquarters Siege Artillery, Line
of Bermuda Hundred, dated January 28, 1865, I have the honor to submit the following report of the part taken by this battery in the engagement with the rebel rams on the 23d and 24th instant:

About 8 p. m. the 23d Fort Brady opened fire; the Cox Ferry batteries replied; I opened, hoping to draw the enemy's fire from Fort
Brady, in order to enable Captain Pierce to serve his guns more rapidly
on the rebel rams, if they were in the river. I was partially successful,
drawing the fire of two 10-inch columbiads and one 8-inch rifled gun.
I expended five case-shot, six percussion-shell, 100-pounder, and five
10-inch mortar shell.

At 10 p. m. Lieutenant Reed, commanding navy picket detachment,
reported to me that a high-pressure side wheel steamer lay at the
obstructions and was attempting to remove them, and that two rams
lay in the channel about 400 yards above. The night was so dark that
I was unable to discover their exact positions excepting by the explosion
of the shell from Battery Parsons. I fired at the rams three 100-pounder
solid shot, at intervals of about fifteen minutes, with what effect I am
unable to tell, and at the steamer nine 10-inch mortar shell, nearly all
of which burst well, annoying the men at work on the obstructions very
much. At 12.30 a. m. the rams dropped down the river to the obstructions where my 100-pounder would not bear on them. At 3 a. m. the
24th one ram dropped down the stream opposite Sleepy Hollow, about
550 yards from the battery, and remained there at anchor about forty-
five minutes. While she lay there one mortar shell, fired at 60 degrees
elevation, charge twelve ounces, without bursting charge, struck her
on the deck without any visible effect; immediately after, however, she
hove up her anchor and changed her position. Thinking it might be
her intention to land a force of marines and attack the battery and
destroy the signal tower, I posted the supernumerary men (about thirty),
with muskets, near the wharf, to prevent any boats landing. The
ram, after dropping down stream about 100 yards, changed her course
and steamed up the river out of sight; not being able to discover her
position I ceased firing until daylight. While she lay opposite Sleepy
Hollow I fired at her nineteen mortar shell, at 60 degrees elevation,
without bursting charge; I cannot state positively that but one struck
her. The firing was very accurate, all the shell striking within a radius

---

On these two pages is the report of Lieutenant E. P. Mason found in the 128-
volume set, *Official Records of the Union and Confederate Armies in the War of the
Rebellion*. In Mason's own words he tells how he directed the cannon fire that
helped turn back the attacking Rebel fleet on the James River in January 1865.
Such a report by one of your ancestors may also be in these volumes.

of ten yards. Soon after daylight I discovered the rams in the channel, about 2,000 yards distant, and partially covered by the bank of the river and a grove of trees. I again opened and fired from the 100-pounder six case-shot, three percussion, and twelve solid shot, and from the mortars thirty-one shell; four solid shot, one percussion, two case-shot, and two mortar shells struck the rams. From this point the only visible damage was by the case-shot, which perforated the smoke-stacks; the percussion-shell burst against her side. The solid shot did not appear to penetrate—some of them after striking rolled back into the water, others ricochetted beyond.

I also fired after daylight at the land batteries (not being able to bear on the rams), with the 100-pounder, eleven case-shot. At about 12 m. the rams succeeded in getting off the bar and steamed around the bend. During the morning of the 24th the battery received the fire of three 10-inch columbiads, one 8-inch and one 7-inch rifled gun.

No casualties occurred.

The men behaved with the utmost coolness and served the pieces with skill and alacrity.

I am, very respectfully, your obedient servant,

E. P. MASON,
First Lieut., First Regiment Connecticut Arty., Comdg. Battery.

Lieut. CHARLES A. TRUESDELL,
Adjutant First Connecticut Artillery.

No. 17.

Report of Lieut. John O'Brien, First Connecticut Heavy Artillery,
commanding Battery No. 4, of operations March 25.

BATTERY NO. 4,
Before Petersburg, Va., March 26, 1865.

LIEUTENANT: I have the honor to submit the following report of the part sustained by Company I, First Connecticut Artillery, the garrison of Battery No. 4, during the engagement of yesterday:

At 4 o'clock in the morning I heard firing on the line near Battery No. 10, but I supposed it was wholly confined to the pickets. At 5.30, an hour and a half later, I saw indications that an advance had been made by the enemy upon our lines near Battery No. 10. I had the company under arms and made arrangements for a defense, when I received orders to open on the enemy, who were now in possession of Fort Stedman and Battery No. 10; these orders were received at daylight. I fired 130 rounds of percussion and 6 rounds of time-fuse shell, nearly all of which were thrown into an advancing column of the enemy, which was in rear of the last-named work. About fifteen shell were thrown into the Chesterfield battery. This battery opened upon Battery No. 5 and the line of works near it, and six shell were thrown into a retreating column of the enemy when it was on the plain in front of Battery No. 9. Fearing an advance, in case of the failure of a pending charge by our forces, fired only when the enemy's troops were in sight, having only about 100 rounds for each piece (three pieces).

I am, sir, very respectfully, your obedient servant,

JOHN O'BRIEN,
First Lieut., First Connecticut Artillery, Comdg. Battery No. 4.

Lieut. W. S. MALONY,
A. A. A. G., Siege Batteries, Before Petersburg, Va.

On the practical side, a name and regiment increases the cash value of an antique. A traceable soldier's name on a revolver will add at least one-third to its value and will easily double the price of a sword, whether enlisted man's or officer's. As an example, several years ago I purchased two swords from a large antique weapons dealer in the East. The sword with the name of the owner, Captain Robert P. Barry, was worth about $500. An almost identical sword, but with no name or other identifying mark, was worth around $300. These prices are now out of date, but the large price gap between the identifiable and the unknown will remain the same and in all probability will widen in the years to come.

A knowledge of the techniques of Civil War research may be the only way you can acquire a truly fine antique at a bargain-basement price. Suppose, in an antique shop, you have found a Union officer's sword with a name inscribed on the hilt. Now, neither you nor the dealer has

Two nearly identical Union officers' swords. The sword inscribed
"Capt. Robert P. Barry" was found to have a traceable history so is worth at
least twice as much as the uninscribed weapon. Its history was a bit hard to trace
because of the scant inscription. Here *Heitmans' Historical Register and
Dictionary of the United States Army* came in very handy.

ever heard of the man. With a basic knowledge of how to search out a name, you can, within a few hours or at the very most within one or two weeks, come up with an answer as to who the man was. The fact may be that this unknown man entered the war as lieutenant but finished as a general. He may never have risen above the rank of lieutenant but may have lived and died a hero's death with that sword in his hand, or he may have been an aide to General Grant or General Sherman. Then again, he may have been a shabby traitor, as the original owner of a sword of a friend once proved to be, or perhaps he was a nobody with a record of practically no interest. He may even be a fictitious character whose name was inscribed on a weapon simply to defraud a buyer. The possibilities are endless, but in any case, you will want to know.

Not long ago, at one of those small-town antique shows where you expect to find nothing, I saw an inconspicuous Colt cap-and-ball six-shooter sticking out of a timeworn holster. There was nothing unusual about it except an inscription engraved on the brass backstrap of the gun, "Francis Preston Blair, Jr.," in beautiful script and under that in bold block letters "St. Louis Mo." The owner of the gun did not know who Blair was. As a historian, I knew that Francis Preston Blair was a famous politician and close friend of Andrew Jackson. The "Jr.," however, failed to ring a bell. A quick twenty-minute trip home and there was Francis Preston Blair, Jr., listed, with photographs, in every major reference book on my library shelf. Fortified with these facts and figures, I bought the gun.

At left is Francis Preston Blair, Jr., Major General commanding the Fifteenth and Seventeenth Corps under Sherman, friend of Lincoln, senator and congressman from Missouri, and the Democratic nominee for Vice-President of the United States in 1868.
Courtesy of the Library of Congress

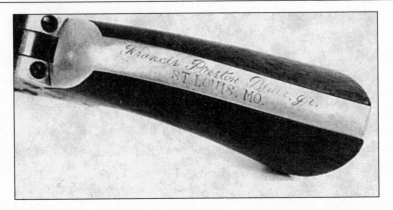

Above is Blair's Colt revolver that went unnoticed and unsold on a
dealer's table until it was identified and bought by a collector who
knew how to trace the name on the backstrap.

Blair is one of Missouri's most famous men. A close friend of Lincoln,
and both a United States representative and a senator, he was the politi-
cal leader responsible for holding Missouri in the Union. He served as a
major general of the Fifteenth and Seventeenth Corps in Sherman's Army
that marched through Georgia, and he ended his long career by being
nominated as the Democratic Vice-Presidential candidate in the election
of 1868.

With a knowledge of where to look, I was able to buy a priceless antique gun—really a museum piece—for very little. Had the dealer from
whom I bought that gun been able to identify the name as I did, you
can imagine the profit he could have had. My case was not really unusual. Countless valuable and identifiable antiques exchange hands at low
prices or go unnoticed and unsold because of the ignorance of buyers
and sellers of, or their indifference to, the fact that names can be traced—
and with no great difficulty at that.

As for you hardened collectors of soldiers' gear who, for reasons of
time or opportunity or whatever, have never tried to master historical
research beyond writing to the National Archives, cheer up! With this
book as a starting guide, the next time your neighbor hefts your inscribed Colt .44 Army revolver, comments on its great weight, and says,
as you are braced from long experience to hear: "Boy, if that old gun
could only talk!" you can take him by the arm, lead him to a comfortable
chair, and *make that old gun talk!*

The National Archives

THOUSANDS UPON THOUSANDS of beginning researchers believe there are no more complete records than those held by the United States Bureau of Archives and Records in Washington, D.C. There is a lot of truth to this. These archives include nearly a million cubic feet of records holding every conceivable type of information, carefully collected and hoarded by the federal government since the founding of our country. The National Archives are open to all, and it is worth a trip to Washington just to be led around and shown what has been preserved for the ages and is at your disposal.

The archives are a vast and priceless source of history. They are doubly important to the occasional researcher because the federal government has a trained professional staff who will search through the millions of records in order to answer your questions. These people will give you

more information in answer to your mail request than almost any other source. Just a tiny fraction of the Civil War material available from the National Archives includes

1. Compiled military service records for each soldier, whether volunteer or regular, Union or Confederate
2. Most of the compiled Union and Confederate Naval and Marine Corps service records
3. Union pension records for all state volunteers and regulars, Army, Navy, and Marines
4. Court-martial case file records
5. Medical records on individual soldiers
6. Prisoner of war records
7. Draft records
8. Burial records

The truly staggering amount of military records held by the National Archives can best be appreciated by examining two of the archives' books. The first is a description of the archives' Union records by Kenneth W. Munden and Henry P. Beers entitled *Guide to Federal Archives Relating to the Civil War, 1962* National Archives Publication No. 63-1. This book is sometimes temporarily out of print when ordered directly from the archives. If that is the case, you may have to find a copy in a library or used book store. In this excellent book the authors describe in detail each kind of record and where it may be found, including personnel records, records for forts and camps, cavalry bureau records, squadron and flotilla records, Marine Corps records, and so on. The Table of Contents lists well over 140 separate bureaus. Six years later Mr. Beers turned out a second volume, this one about the Confederacy, entitled *Guide to the Archives of the Government of the Confederate States of America,* National Archives Publication No. 68-15.

Since the federal government searchers will do a great deal of looking for you, these books are not really necessary for an average search request. But if you want to squeeze every last drop of information from

your soldier or regiment, these two books are indispensable. They list the type and location of millions of pages of records held not only by the National Archives but by your own and other states and by museums, colleges, universities, and the like. What a lifesaver they are for professional Civil War historians! To obtain these two books write to

National Archives
Publications Services Branch
8th and Pennsylvania Avenue, NW
Washington, D.C. 20408

The archives have a fine publication that does not relate specifically to the Civil War as does Beers and Munden. The book's title is *Guide to Genealogical Research in the National Archives.* It is an outline of the complete span of records useful for tracing any ancestor, military and nonmilitary, from colonial times to the present. It directs you to records concerning civilians during wartime, American Indians, black Americans, merchant seamen, government employees, land records, claims and court records, the census, passenger arrivals, naturalization records, regular army, navy, and marine records, pension records, bounty, land, and map records, and the list goes on. Remember, however, that for Civil War records, Beers and Munden's books are still the most complete—nothing beats them, nothing!

To begin a mail-order search at the national level, you must supply some information. You must provide the searchers with the last name of your soldier or sailor, and it is highly desirable to know his first initial, or better still, his full name. You must also know his military unit: the First Connecticut Heavy Artillery, Seventh New York Infantry, Twenty-sixth Mississippi Infantry, U.S.S. *Monitor*, C.S.S. *Alabama* or whatever it may be. The government archivists will not, for love or money, search for Private Henry Jones, Ohio Infantry, and they will be reluctant to look for Private Smith, Twenty-eighth Mississippi, since there may possibly be fifteen Henry Joneses and two hundred Private Smiths. Falling short of a complete or partially complete name, and lacking the soldier's military

unit, you must fall back on the alternatives outlined further on in this book. Assuming that you have a name and military outfit, your next step is to telephone or address a short letter to

National Archives and Records Administration
General Reference Branch (NNRG-P)
7th and Pennsylvania Avenue, NW
Washington, D.C. 20408
(202) 501-5170

Make a brief statement of whom you wish to research and request five or six sets of NATF Form 80 so that you may order photocopies concerning your veteran. This is the form that is used for researching any veteran from the Revolution to the Spanish American War.

In about three weeks to a month you will receive your NATF 80 forms. This form changes quite often. The present one has an original white form with three copies beneath it. When you write heavily with a ball-point pen or type on the original, the forms underneath become automatic copies. Take two complete forms and fill out the first white copy, checking that you want pension records. On the second white copy check that you want military records. Remember that each white form is a separate request and that you will be billed for each as a separate order.

Though the government's procedure changes from time to time, at the present writing you need send no money with your NATF 80 form. Everything you send will soon be returned to you. If they find some records, they will tell you so and you must send the money requested together with the forms. If they find no records, it will cost you nothing but the postage involved in the writing. What you pay if records are found is a real bargain, since the cost to the government for your search is much more than that. But some agency in that vast bureaucracy of ours pays the difference in a subsidy to the archives. The directions on the form will tell you to send one NATF Form 80 set to the government for each soldier you wish searched.

What may not be quite so clear to the beginning researcher is that the record of a man's military service in any one organization is wholly separate from the record of his service in any other organization. This means

that if your ancestor joined the Sixteenth New York and later transferred to the Twenty-eighth, your NATF Form 80 request will get you his service in only the one unit you requested, the Sixteenth New York. It will take another NATF form set to get his service record with the Twenty-eighth New York. You will be billed for each form answered.

Send the forms and see what your inquiry brings. If your soldier was an enlisted volunteer, the chances are that not more than ten pages of records exist. If, however, your soldier was an officer, there is a much better chance that there are extensive records. This is especially true if he was a commanding officer, an inspector, a commissary officer, a regimental adjutant, a surgeon, or perhaps a chaplain. Where officers are concerned, there may be thirty more pages of which you are totally unaware and of which no one will tell you unless you inquire. If you have reason to believe from the rank and position of responsibility of your soldier that there may be more than ten pages, the best approach is to staple a note or write across the top of your NATF form, "Send all military records." Then take out another white form and across the top write, "Send all pension records." With luck, your requests will be returned to you with an estimate of the cost of the additional records. You will never get research done less expensively, no matter what the extra cost!

If the military records indicate that great-grandfather was given a general court-martial (a secret the family has successfully hidden for a hundred years or so), reach for another NATF Form 80, fill it out, and staple a note or write across the top, "Please send all court-martial records." You do this because the military records do not include court-martial records, nor will you be informed of their existence unless you request them. Unfortunately for descendants, Confederate court-martial records are almost nonexistent, so there is little need to bother asking for them.

This is not the end of the use of NATF Form 80. If you either suspect, or the pension or military records show, that your soldier was sick, wounded, or disabled in any way, reach for yet another NATF Form 80, fill it out, and staple a note or write across the top, "Please send complete medical records." You must do this because, as in the case of court-martial records, medical records are not included in the military records, and researchers in the archives will not tell you that they exist unless you specifically request them.

NATIONAL ARCHIVES ORDER FOR COPIES OF VETERANS RECORDS

Dear Researcher,

Before completing the form, please read both sides of this page for ordering instructions and general information about the types of records that can be ordered with this form. Mail order photocopying service by using this form is available **ONLY** from *General Reference Branch (NNRG–P), National Archives and Records Administration, 7th and Pennsylvania Avenue NW., Washington, DC 20408.* For more information, please write to us at the address above.

IMPORTANT INFORMATION ABOUT YOUR ORDER

The success of our search depends on the completeness and accuracy of the information you provide in blocks 3–18 on this form. Please note that each NATF Form 80 is handled separately. When you send more than one form at a time, you may not receive all of your replies at the same time.

Military service records rarely contain family information. Pension application files generally are most useful to those who are doing genealogical research and contain the most complete information regarding a man's military career. We suggest that you first request copies of a man's pension file. You should request copies of a bounty–land warrant file or a military record only when no pension file exists. If the veteran's service was during the Revolutionary War, bounty–land warrant applications have been consolidated with pension application papers. You can obtain both files by requesting the pension file only.

We will copy complete compiled military service and bounty–land application files. When we are unable to provide copies of all pension documents because of the size of a pension application file, we will send copies of the documents we think will be most useful to you for genealogical purposes. Many of the documents in these files are repetitive or administrative in nature. You may order copies of all remaining documents in a file by making a specific request. We will notify you of the cost of the additional copies.

Do NOT use this form to request photocopies of records relating to service in World War I or II, or subsequent service. Write to: *National Personnel Records Center (Military Records), NARA, 9700 Page Boulevard, St. Louis, MO 63132.*

INSTRUCTIONS FOR COMPLETING THIS FORM

Use a separate NATF Form 80 for each file that you request. Remove this instruction sheet. You must complete blocks 3–7 or we cannot search for the file. Print your name (last, first, middle) and address in the block provided at the bottom of the form, which is your mailing label. The information must be legible on all copies. Keep the PINK copy of the form for your records. Mail the remaining three pages of the form to: *General Reference Branch (NNRG–P), National Archives and Records Administration, 7th and Pennsylvania Avenue NW., Washington, DC 20408.* **DO NOT SEND PAYMENT WITH THIS FORM.** When we search your order, we will make photocopies of records that relate to your request. For credit card orders, we will mail the copies immediately. For other types of orders, we will invoice you for the cost of these copies and hold them until we receive your payment.

**SEE THE REVERSE OF THIS PAGE FOR DESCRIPTIONS OF
THE TYPES OF RECORDS THAT CAN BE ORDERED WITH THIS FORM.**

Above and on the opposite page are instruction pages
that arrive with each NATF 80 form.

TYPES OF RECORDS THAT CAN BE ORDERED WITH THIS FORM

PENSION APPLICATION FILES

Pension application files, based on Federal (not State) service before World War I, usually include an official statement of the veteran's military service, as well as information of a personal nature. Pensions based on military service for the Confederate States of America were authorized by some Southern States but not by the Federal Government until 1959. Inquiries about State pensions should be addressed to the State archives or equivalent agency at the capital of the veteran's State of residence after the war.

BOUNTY-LAND WARRANT APPLICATION FILES

Bounty-land warrant application files are based on Federal (not State) service before 1856. Documents in a bounty-land warrant application file are similar to those in a pension application file. In addition, these files usually give the veteran's age and place of residence at the time the application was made.

MILITARY SERVICE RECORDS

Military service records are based on service in the UNITED STATES ARMY (officers who served before June 30, 1917, and enlisted men who served before October 31, 1912); NAVY (officers who served before 1903 and enlisted men who served before 1886); MARINE CORPS (officers who served before 1896 and enlisted men who served before 1905); and CONFEDERATE ARMED FORCES (officers and enlisted men, 1861–65). In addition to persons who served in regular forces raised by the Federal Government, volunteers fought in various wars chiefly in the Federal Government's interest from the Revolutionary War through the Philippine Insurrection, 1775–1902.

Compilations of information concerning most military service performed by individuals in volunteer organizations during the 19th and early 20th centuries are available, but such records were not compiled for Regular Army officers who served before 1863 and for Regular Army enlisted men and Navy and Marine Corps personnel who served during most of the 19th century. Records pertaining to such service are scattered among many files and generally contain few details concerning a man's service. We cannot undertake the research necessary to locate all such documents. If you request a military service record, we will copy the documents that best summarize the veteran's service.

The record of an individual's service in any one organization is entirely separate from his record of service in another organization. We are unable to establish accurately the identity of individuals of the same name who served in different organizations. If you know that an individual served in more than one organization and you desire copies of all of the military service records, submit a separate form for the service record in each organization.

Discharge certificates are not usually included as a part of a compiled military service record. Before 1944, Army regulations allowed the preparation of an original discharge certificate only, which was given to the soldier. Confederate soldiers in service at the time of surrender did not receive discharge certificates. They were given paroles, and these paroles became the property of the soldier.

NATIONAL ARCHIVES
ORDER FOR COPIES OF VETERANS RECORDS
(See Instructions page before completing this form)

DATE RECEIVED IN NNRG

INDICATE BELOW THE TYPE OF FILE DESIRED AND THE METHOD OF PAYMENT PREFERRED.

1. FILE TO BE SEARCHED
(Check one box only)
☐ PENSION
☐ BOUNTY–LAND WARRANT APPLICATION *(Service before 1856 only)*
☐ MILITARY

2. PAYMENT METHOD *(Check one box only)*

☐ CREDIT CARD *(VISA or MasterCard) for IMMEDIATE SHIPMENT of copies*

Account Number:

Exp. Date:

Signature:

Daytime Phone:

☐ **BILL ME** *(No Credit Card)*

REQUIRED MINIMUM IDENTIFICATION OF VETERAN – MUST BE COMPLETED OR YOUR ORDER CANNOT BE SERVICED

3. VETERAN *(Give last, first, and middle names)*

4. BRANCH OF SERVICE IN WHICH HE SERVED
☐ ARMY ☐ NAVY ☐ MARINE CORPS

5. STATE FROM WHICH HE SERVED

6. WAR IN WHICH, OR DATES BETWEEN WHICH, HE SERVED

7. IF SERVICE WAS CIVIL WAR,
☐ UNION ☐ CONFEDERATE

PLEASE PROVIDE THE FOLLOWING ADDITIONAL INFORMATION, IF KNOWN

8. UNIT IN WHICH HE SERVED *(Name of regiment or number, company, etc, name of ship)*

9. IF SERVICE WAS ARMY, ARM IN WHICH HE SERVED
☐ INFANTRY ☐ CAVALRY ☐ ARTILLERY

If other, specify:

Rank
☐ OFFICER ☐ ENLISTED

10. KIND OF SERVICE
☐ VOLUNTEERS ☐ REGULARS

11. PENSION/BOUNTY–LAND FILE NO.

12. IF VETERAN LIVED IN A HOME FOR SOLDIERS, GIVE LOCATION *(City and State)*

13. PLACE(S) VETERAN LIVED AFTER SERVICE

14. DATE OF BIRTH

15. PLACE OF BIRTH *(City, County, State, etc.)*

18. NAME OF WIDOW OR OTHER CLAIMANT

16. DATE OF DEATH

17. PLACE OF DEATH *(City, County, State, etc.)*

NATIONAL ARCHIVES TRUST FUND BOARD   NATF Form 80 (rev. 10–93)

DO NOT WRITE BELOW – SPACE IS FOR OUR REPLY TO YOU

☐ **NO--We were unable to locate the file you requested above. No payment is required.**

DATE SEARCHED   SEARCHER

☐ **REQUIRED MINIMUM IDENTIFICATION OF VETERAN WAS NOT PROVIDED.** Please complete blocks 3 (give full name), 4, 5, 6, and 7 and resubmit your order.

☐ **A SEARCH WAS MADE BUT THE FILE YOU REQUESTED ABOVE WAS NOT FOUND.** When we do not find a record for a veteran, this does not mean that he did not serve. You may be able to obtain information about him from the archives of the State from which he served.

☐ See attached forms, leaflets, or information sheets.

☐ **YES--We located the file you requested above. We have made copies from the file for you. The cost for these copies is $10.**

DATE SEARCHED   SEARCHER

FILE DESIGNATION

Make your check or money order payable to NATIONAL ARCHIVES TRUST FUND. Do not send cash. Return this form and your payment in the enclosed envelope to:

NATIONAL ARCHIVES TRUST FUND
P.O. BOX 100221
ATLANTA, GA 30384-0221

PLEASE NOTE: We will hold these copies awaiting receipt of payment for only 45 days from the date completed, which is stamped below. After that time, you must submit another form to obtain photocopies of the file.

THIS IS YOUR MAILING LABEL.

NAME *(Last, First, MI)*

A949943

STREET

PRESS FIRMLY.

CITY, STATE

ZIP CODE

INVOICE/REPLY COPY – DO NOT DETACH

The white master copy of form NATF 80. This is the form with which you begin all your searches in the National Archives.

A 85 N.Y.
Chauncey S. Aldrich
Rank Adjutant Reg't N. Y. Infantry.
Appears on
Field and Staff Muster Roll
for Jany & Feby, 1862
Present or absent Present

A 85 N.Y.
Chauncey S Aldrich
Capt, Co. B, 85 Reg't N. Y. Infantry.
Appears on
Company Muster Roll
for Sept and Oct, 1863
Present or absent Present

A 85 N.Y.
Chauncey S. Aldrich
Adjt, Co. ...., 85 Reg't N. Y. Infantry.
Appears on **Special Muster Roll**
for Aug 18, 1862
Present or absent Present

A 85 N.Y.
C S Aldrich
Capt, Co. B, 85 Reg't N. Y. Infantry.
Appears on **Regimental Return**
for Oct, 1863.
Present or absent Present

A 85 N.Y.
Chauncey S Aldrich
1 Lt, Co. B, 85 Reg't N. Y. Infantry.
Age 27 years.
Appears on
Company Muster-in Roll

A 85 N.Y.
Chauncey S. Aldrich
Capt., Co. B, 85 Reg't N. Y. Infantry.
Appears on a
Detachment Muster Roll
of the organization named above
for Jan & Feb, 1864.
Station Canandaigua N.Y.
Present or absent Present.
Stoppage, $ ...... 100 for
Due Gov't, $ ...... 100 for
Remarks: In Command of Company until Feb. 16th 1864 — Detached on recruiting service Feb. 17 1864 by Special Order No. 48. Hd. Qrs. Dept. Virginia & North Carolina
Bookmark:
(844) A J Anderson Copyist.

A 85 N.Y.
S. C. Aldrich
Rank Adjt, 85 Reg't N. Y. Infantry.
Appears on
Field and Staff Muster-out Roll
of the organization named above. Roll dated
New Berne N.C., June 27 1865.
Muster-out to date * ~~June 27, 1865~~
Last paid to ...., 186 .

A 85 N.Y.
Chauncey S. Aldrich
1 Lt, Co. ...., 85 Reg't N. Y. Infantry.
Appears on an
Individual Muster-out Roll

A 85 N.Y.
Chauncey S. Aldrich
Capt, Co. B, 85 Reg't N. Y. Infantry.
Appears on **Co. Muster-out Roll**, dated
New Berne, N.C. June 27, 1865.
Muster-out to date ...., 186 .
Last paid to ...., 186 .
Clothing account:
Last settled ...., 186 ; drawn since $ 100
Due soldier $ ...... 100; due U. S. $ 100
Am't for cloth'g in kind or money adv'd $ 100
Due U. S. for arms, equipments, &c., $ 100
Bounty paid $ ...... 100; due $ 100
Remarks: Promoted to 1st Lieut. Aug. 26, 61. Promoted to Capt. Aug. 21, 63. Discharged Dec. 15, 64 under provisions of paragraph 3 Circular 75, A.G. Office Series of 64
Book mark:
(861) Jno. J. Bell, Jr. Copyist.

A 85 N.Y.
Chauncey S Aldrich
Adjutant 85 Reg N Y Vols
Return
of the Post of Newport News, Va.,
for the month of September, 1862,
dated Oct 3, 1862,
shows the following with regard to the person named above:

Above are ten different types of muster rolls—a small example of the variety of data available from the National Archives.
Courtesy of the National Archives

It was in just such a way that I uncovered the detailed story of a Colt .31-caliber six-shooter with "H. Gaebel, N.Y. 7th L.V." engraved on the backstrap. In New York City eleven days after Confederate General Beauregard had sent the first shell bursting over Fort Sumter in Charleston Harbor to begin the Civil War, Prussian-born engineer F. A. H. Gaebel was mustered into the Seventh New York Volunteer Infantry as Captain of Company A. Two months later Gaebel was leading his company against Confederate fortifications at Big Bethel, a few miles west of Newport News, Virginia. On March 8-9, 1862, during the time of the famous battle between the *Monitor* and the *Merrimac,* Gaebel and his regiment lined the northern shore of the James River and showered the Confederate ironclad monster, *Merrimac,* with rifle balls in the futile hope of doing some accidental damage to the ship's crew. In the following months the Seventh, as a part of General McClellan's vast invading army, pushed the Rebel forces behind the siege lines of Richmond.

By now Gaebel's bravery had caused him to be promoted to major. For three more months and five more battles—Peach Orchard, Savage Station, White Oak Swamp, Malvern Hill (where he was breveted for bravery in action), and South Mountain—Major Gaebel's luck held, and for all his recklessness he remained untouched by shell or bullet. Then, on September 16, at the Battle of Antietam, called Sharpsburg by the Rebels, a Confederate Minié ball struck him down for the first time. On December 13, not yet fully recovered from his Antietam wound, he led his regiment up the shell- and shrapnel-swept Marye's Heights at Fredericksburg. On this bloody slope over 7,000 Union soldiers were to lie dead or wounded. A medical report from the National Archives shows that Gaebel's index finger was broken when a bullet smashed his sword from his hand. A musket ball pierced his body, and a shell fragment tore a hole in his leg. Totally disabled but still alive and now a lieutenant colonel, he was sent back to his native New York City to convalesce. Several months later he left a bride of one month to return to duty with the Seventh until it was mustered out of service in May 1863. Too crippled for active service, he volunteered as a major in the Sixteenth Veteran's Reserve Corps, a regiment made up of invalids like himself. As the commanding officer of this group, he spent the remainder of the war chasing draft dodgers, escaped prisoners, and Southern sympathizers in the

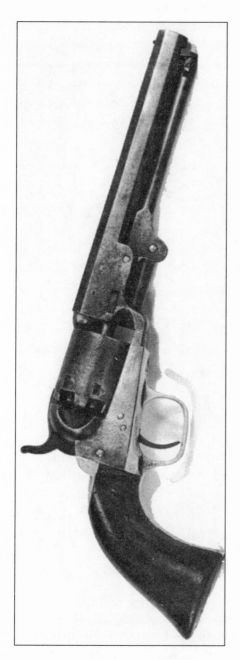

Colt .31-caliber six-shooter carried by Colonel H. Gaebel when he led his
regiment in a disastrous charge up Marye's Heights in the battle of
Fredericksburg, Virginia, December 11-15, 1862. This information was found
by a special request for medical records in the National Archives—an easy
search because all the necessary information was plainly engraved
on the pictured backstrap.

This order directs Lt. Col. F. A. H. Gaebel of the 16th Veteran's Reserve Corps to investigate persons suspected of being involved in the assassination of Abraham Lincoln. Such a find makes a search unusually rewarding, especially if the soldier was a close relative.

Courtesy of the National Archives

G. | 7th | **N. Y.**

F. A. H. Gaebel

Rank *Lt. Col.*, 7. Reg't N. Y. Infantry.

Appears on

Field and Staff Muster Roll

for *Jan. & Feb.*, 1863.

Joined for duty and enrolled:

When *Sept. 28*, 1862.*

Where *Camp near Falmouth Va*

Period .... years.*

Present or absent *Absent*

Stoppage, $............ 100 for ....

Due Gov't, $............ 100 for ....

Valuation of horse, $............ 100

Valuation of horse equipments, $............ 100

Remarks: *Wounded in battle of Fredericksburg Oct. 13. In Hospital at Washington.*

* See enrollment on card from muster-in roll.

Book mark : ....

E. E. Rankin,
Copyist.

(857c)

Vet. Res. Corps. Nov 12/63.
Brevetted Lt. Col. U. S. V.
Dec. 10/64.
Gunshot in right side, gunshot in hilt of sword breaking index finger, piece of shell cutting the right leg. — degree of disability Total.

JAN.-5. 30452848 1894.

Above is an officer's muster roll from the National Archives for Lt. Col. F. A. H. Gaebel, 7th New York Infantry. It shows that he was "Wounded in [the] battle of Fredericksburg October 13" and was in the hospital in Washington. Often you can dig deeper beyond such a brief reporting of the facts, as the author did, and come up with the fascinating details, as can be seen by the accompanying report.
Courtesy of the National Archives.

mountains of Pennsylvania. At one time the government records show that he and his regiment were tracking down suspected assassins of Abraham Lincoln. After Appomattox, the federal government honored Gaebel by giving him a first lieutenant's commission in the Forty-fifth Regiment of the regular United States Army. Three years later Gaebel's old war wounds sapped his strength and he died just before Christmas in 1868.

Many aspects of this story were found by using NATF Form 80 forms and requesting medical records in addition to regular military records.

Here, then, is what you may expect from NATF Form 80: for the Union soldier, pension, military, medical, and court-martial records; for the Confederate soldier, as a general rule, military records only. These may include muster rolls, leaves, perhaps a prisoner-of-war record, and a few miscellaneous orders. You will have to turn to the individual state archives for more information on Johnny Reb. The National Archives, however, are the ultimate source for Union military personnel records and for tens of millions of historical facts concerning both the Union and the Confederate armies and navies.

One last hopeful hint in using NATF Form 80. The training and ability of the government's searchers varies considerably. If your form is returned to you with the discouraging message, "We were unable to locate the file you requested," your searcher may have had an off day or been new to the job or whatever. Just send in another set with the same information. Your new request may fall into some expert hands that can find exactly what you were requesting. It has happened to me!

If you have had no luck by this point, a telephone call or a letter to the National Archives and Records Administration, General Reference Branch, 7th and Pennsylvania Avenue, NW, Washington, D.C. 20408, (202) 501-5170, requesting help may give you just the lead you need.

Those of you who have either a microfilm reader or easy access to one will be glad to learn that the National Archives has for sale a *Comprehensive Catalog of National Archives Microfilm*. Here are listed thousands of microfilm rolls of records from the Secretary of War, Judge Advocate's office, Chief Signal Officer, military posts, and navy personnel, to mention only a bare fraction of the entries. These records are not limited to the Civil War but cover all aspects of American history from the Revolu-

tion to well into the twentieth century. If you wish to zero in on military microfilm, there is a 330-page National Archives catalog (paperback) entitled *Military Service Records: A Select Catalog of National Archives Microfilm Publications.* This book covers compiled service records from the Revolution to World War I and from regulars to reserve, navy and marines, as well as land warrants, rendezvous reports, and bounty and pension records. Order it from the National Archives Publications Services Branch listed earlier (see p. 13). The occasional searcher will not often need to use microfilm. A serious Civil War student must not overlook microfilm from the archives if he does not have the time and money to visit Washington himself.

The National Parks Service has begun a huge program called the Civil War Soldier's System. The aim of the project is to have special parts of the army records of every Civil War Soldier, Union or Confederate, available by computer at its Civil War commemorative sites (see Appendix E.) For the time being, sailors and marines will not be included.

Over 5,400,000 records will be available at these sites. Here is instant genealogical gratification and a wonderful opportunity. These records are scheduled to be available in 1996. Remember that state-operated Civil War commemorative sites will not be included initially, and may not be for some time. State parks may enter the program, but it is a matter of time, money, and cooperation.

You won't have to be particularly knowledgeable about computers to operate the system. At any one of the sites, you will be able to sit down at a computer, type in your veteran's name, and get a printout of the following: your soldier's enlisted name or names, some used aliases, his starting and ending rank, his regiment, cross regimental history, including battles fought. There will also be a list of soldiers buried at the park where you are conducting your search. What will not be available at the sites—not for now, anyway—are pension records, prisoner-of-war records, court-martial records, ship's battle records, etc. To get such records, follow the procedures outlined in the National Archives NATF Form (revised October 1993) and the guidelines in this book.

The National Park Service is not trying to duplicate the National Archives out of the genealogy business—that it could never do. Millions upon millions of Civil War records will still be found only in the

National Archives. The National Park Service is just trying to make the basic data readily available to the public at its sites. It will continually add to the data as time passes.

The park service is being aided in its ambitious project by many outside sources. Many local societies of the nationwide Federation of Genealogical Societies are involved, in addition to the well-known Genealogical Society of Utah.

Collecting data will be an endless process, and many hands will be needed to keep the effort going. The National Park Service is looking for volunteers to aid in the gathering, sorting, and distribution of information. Anyone interested and able to operate a computer, preferably an IBM system, may write Civil War Soldier's System, P.O. Box 3385, Salt Lake City, Utah 84110-2385. You will be sent the necessary information to become part of this historic project. Graduate students might consider what it would do for their vita. There are no guarantees, but the experience just might help them to get a better job or to win favorable consideration for an academic program.

The State Archives

A BOTTOMLESS WELL OF INFORMATION the National Archives may be, but there are, nevertheless, countless other sources to which you may turn. Let us go next to the state archives. They are full to the brim with records of servicemen who fought in what many Southerners preferred to call "The War for Southern Independence" and ardent Northerners termed "The War of the Rebellion."

Each state in the nation has archives in which the state's historical treasures and records are kept. Some states, such as Michigan, Virginia, and Georgia, have superb facilities. Others apparently care less for their past or are unable to obtain the necessary funds, and their archives and offers of help reflect this. Varied in quality as the help is, most of the states will be able to add something to your search.

There are a number of advantages that do not seem apparent at first in writing to the state. If you are really anxious for a quick answer to a few basic questions, such as "Does a record of my soldier really exist?" (There are thousands that don't.) "What were his service dates, promotions, and unit?" or "Did he die in the war?" then the state archives are your best bet. A letter addressed to a state government will bring a reply in from

one to three weeks at most. A request to the harassed and understaffed National Archives in Washington will take from one to three months.

If your soldier happens to be a Confederate, it is really essential to write to the state in whose forces he served. Years after the War Between the States was over, the federal government gave pensions to most of those who had fought in the Union armies. But after fighting a long and disastrous war, the federal government was understandably not in the mood to give pensions to soldiers of the Confederacy, so recently the enemy. So it was that Confederate pensions were left to the consciences of the ex-Confederate governments. The result was that each Southern state gave its own individual pensions to its soldiers. When Johnny Rebs sat down in courthouses throughout the South to fill out their pension forms, they were, without realizing it, contributing considerably to the preservation of their wartime history. Years later, to the delight of relatives, collectors, and historians, Confederate pension records proved to be a small mine of information.

As an example, the Louisiana "Soldier's Application for Pension" gives the applicant's age, place of birth, date of enlistment, command and company, and branch of service. It will tell whether the veteran was wounded, where, when, and during what battle, how he was wounded, the nature of the wound, and the attending surgeon. If he was a prisoner of war, the pension application will tell when and how he was released, whether he was paroled or discharged, whether he suffered the loss of an eye or a limb, and whether he was discharged for wounds or disability. It will also tell whether the soldier was at the final surrender or took the oath of allegiance to the United States during the war. It will tell whether he was married, how many children he had, what his occupation was after the war, and whether he owned any real estate. It will even state whether or not he drank. In addition, it will name two comrades and give their addresses.

If the soldier you are tracing, whether Union or Confederate, was in the State Militia and not a volunteer, he will have no records in Washington. They will be only in the state archives.

A word about the difference between the State Militia and the State Volunteers. The militia was a state-organized and controlled citizen army,

DECLARATION FOR ORIGINAL INVALID PENSION.

State of New York,
County of *New York* }ss.:

On this *3rd* day of *December* 187*9*, personally appeared before me _____ CLERK OF *N. Y. Supreme* COURT, a duly authorized officer of a Court of Record in the County and State aforesaid, *Thomas Cummings* who being duly sworn according to law, declares:—That he is the identical person who enlisted under the name *of aforesaid* in the military service of the United States at *New York* on the *21st* day of *May, 1861* in Company *36°* of the *82nd* Regiment, *New York* in the war of 1861, and was honorably discharged on the *2d* day of *June, 1864.*

That while in the service aforesaid, and in the line of his duty, he *was wounded in the right thigh, about midway between the knee and hip, at the battle of Gettysburg, Pa., on July 2nd 1863. The ball entered in front, towards the outside of the leg and passed straight through from front to rear. He was treated for two or three days in White Building Hospital, Baltimore Md, was then furloughed for thirty days, and the furlough was extended for five days by the Medical Director at New York City. At the time of his wounding he was Captain of the above company.*

That he has not been employed in the Military or Naval Service of the United States, otherwise than as above stated.

He has never received or applied for pension, for which he now applies, under act of Congress approved July 14th, 1862, and amendments, by reason of the disability above stated.

He hereby constitutes and appoints *Theo. D. Valentine* No. 111 Nassau Street, New York, his Attorney to prosecute this claim.

A New York State Invalid Pension form showing that Capt. Thomas Cummings of the 82nd Regiment was "wounded in the right thigh midway between the knee and hip at the battle of Gettysburg, Pa. . . . The Ball entered in front, towards the outside of the leg and passed straight through from front to rear." Many veterans have such details of their wounds recorded in the National Archives in Washington.

Courtesy of the National Archives

now called the National Guard, whose main purpose was to protect the citizens and property within a particular state. The militia had no connection with either the Confederate or Union governments. During the Civil War both Union and Confederate militia troops often left their state to fight for their country. However, almost all of the vast armies on both sides were made up mostly of State Volunteer regiments, raised and turned over to Abe Lincoln or Jeff Davis. For those tracing earlier soldiers who were in militia units in the War of 1812 and during the Indian Wars, if their units were not officially taken into the army, their records will be found in the state files only. Revolutionary soldiers are the exception. All the available records of soldiers, sailors, and marines of Washington's troops and ships can be found in the National Archives.

After the war, a number of Confederate state officials, still bitter and unreconstructed, deliberately withheld records requested by the federal authorities. So here is another reason why more information is not available in Washington.

Some years ago the federal government began reproducing on microfilm all the veterans' personnel records held in the National Archives. This giant task began and ended with Southern soldiers. It included not only records of Johnny Rebs but those of Southern men who were against disunion and marched north to join the Blue ranks. So far, the Northern personnel records have not been reproduced, nor are there any plans to do so. Libraries and state archives throughout the South have purchased copies of the microfilmed records, and they are available to you on request at about the same cost as those of the National Archives. Check the list of addresses in Appendix A to locate those records nearest you. You will probably save a month or perhaps two that you would otherwise spend in waiting for replies from Washington.

The federal government has also compiled an index to these Southern records which you may find useful. It will give all the recorded names and regiments of all the soldiers from Southern states who fought in either army. With this index you can establish whether records exist on any soldier of Southern origin. This index has been sold all over the United States to colleges, universities, state and local historical societies, and archives. Call the large library nearest you to see if it has a copy of the index.

Most of the states involved in the Civil War will send a brief abstract of a particular soldier at no cost to you. Those states that have the staff and equipment will usually go into a deeper search at fifteen cents or more a page for duplicated records. From those states equipped to help you, you may get quite a bit on individual soldiers and military units. I must sadly relate that such states as Louisiana, which will go beyond summaries in response to a mail request for information, are growing fewer by the year. Almost all the states are quite eager for you to come and look for yourself into their extensive archives and use them. Lack of money for a research staff, however, is gradually limiting mail searches. Many of the states, such as Michigan, North Carolina, and Arkansas, will send you special pamphlets on the contents of their archives.

Remember, when tracing Yankees or Rebels, a letter will get better results than a hasty card. Send your inquiry to one of the state addresses given below:

ALABAMA
Alabama Department
  of Archives and History
624 Washington Avenue
Montgomery, Alabama 36130
(205) 242-4361

ALASKA
Alaska State Archives and
  Records Management Services
141 Willoughby Avenue
Juneau, Alaska 99801
(907) 465-2275

ARIZONA
Arizona State Archives
1700 West Washington
Phoenix, AZ 85007
(602) 542-4159

ARKANSAS
Arkansas History Commission
One Capitol Mall
Little Rock, Arkansas 72201
(501) 682-6900

CALIFORNIA
California State Archives
1020 0 Street
Sacramento, California 95814

COLORADO
Division of State
  Archives and Public Records
1313 Sherman Street
Room 1-820
Denver, Colorado 80203
(303) 866-2055

CONNECTICUT
History and Genealogy Unit
231 Capitol Avenue
Hartford, Connecticut 06106
(203) 566-3690

DELAWARE
Delaware State Archives
Hall of Records
Dover, Delaware 19901
(302) 739-5318

FLORIDA
Bureau of Archives
  and Records Management
R. A. Gray Building
500 South Bronough Street
Tallahassee, Florida 32399-0250
(904) 487-2073

GEORGIA
Georgia Department
  of Archives and History
Civil War Records
Section 330 Capitol Avenue, SW
Atlanta, Georgia 30334
(404) 656-2350

HAWAII
Hawaii State Archives
Iolani Palace Grounds
Honolulu, Hawaii 96813
(808) 586-0329

IDAHO
Genealogy Library
325 West State Street
Boise, Idaho 83702
(208) 334-2305

ILLINOIS
Illinois State Archives
Archives Building
Capitol Complex
Springfield, Illinois 62756
(217) 782-4682

INDIANA
Indiana State Archives
  Indiana Commission
  on Public Records
140 North Senate Avenue,
Room 117
Indianapolis, Indiana 46204
(317) 232-3660 ext. 3737

IOWA
State Historical Society of Iowa
  Library and Archives
600 East Locust
Des Moines, Iowa 50319
(515) 281-6200

KANSAS
Kansas State Historical Society
120 Southwest 10th Street
Topeka, Kansas 66612
(913) 296-3251

KENTUCKY
Kentucky Department
  of Library and Archives
Division of Archives
  and Records Management
300 Coffeetree Road
Frankfort, Kentucky 40602
(502) 875-7000

LOUISIANA
State of Louisiana
Secretary of State
Division of Archives,
  Records Management,
  and History
3851 Essen Lane
P.O. Box 94125
Baton Rouge, Louisiana
  70804-9125
(504) 922-1200

MAINE
Maine State Archives
Station 84
Augusta, Maine 04333
(207) 287-5790

MARYLAND
Maryland State Archives
350 Rowe Boulevard
Annapolis, Maryland 21401
(410) 974-3914

MASSACHUSETTS
Massachusetts State Archives
Columbia Point
220 Morrissey Boulevard
Boston, Massachussetts 02125
(617) 727-2816

MICHIGAN
Michigan State Archives
717 West Allegan Street
Lansing, Michigan 48918-1805
(517) 373-1408

MINNESOTA
Minnesota Historical Society
  Division of Archives and
  Manuscripts
Reference Division
345 Kellogg Boulevard West
St. Paul, Minnesota 55102-1906
(612) 296-6980

MISSISSIPPI
Mississippi Department of
  Archives and History
P.O. Box 571
Jackson, Mississippi 39205
(601) 359-6875

MISSOURI
Office of the Adjutant General
2302 Militia Drive
Jefferson City, Missouri
  65101-1203
(314) 526-9500

MONTANA
Montana Historical Society
  Division of Archives
  and Manuscripts
225 North Roberts Street
P.O. Box 201201
Helena, Montana 59620-1201
(406) 444-2681

NEBRASKA
Nebraska State Historical Society
  State Archives Division
P.O. Box 82554
Lincoln, Nebraska 68501
(402) 471-3270

NEVADA
Nevada State Library and Archives
Capitol Complex
Carson City, Nevada 89710
(702) 687-5160

NEW HAMPSHIRE
Division of Records and Archives
71 South Fruit Street
Concord, New Hampshire 03301
(603) 271-2236

NEW JERSEY
Department of State
  Division of Archives
  and Records Management
Archives Section
185 West State Street, CN 307
Trenton, New Jersey 08625
(609) 292-6260

NEW MEXICO
State Records Center and Archives
404 Montezuma
Santa Fe, New Mexico 87503
(505) 827-7332

NEW YORK:
New York State Archives
Room llD40
Cultural Education Center
Empire State Plaza
Albany, New York 12230
(518) 474-8955

NORTH CAROLINA
North Carolina Department
  of Cultural Resources
North Carolina State Archives
109 East Jones Street
Raleigh, North Carolina 27601
(919) 733-3952

NORTH DAKOTA
State Historical Society
  of North Dakota
612 East Boulevard
Bismarck, North Dakota 58505
(701) 328-2666

*OHIO
Ohio State Historical Society
The Archives Library
1982 Velma Avenue
Columbus, Ohio 43211-2497
(614) 297-2300

*No research by mail. Will send list of genealogists on request.

OKLAHOMA
Oklahoma Department
 of Libraries
Archives and Records Division
200 Northeast 18th Street
Oklahoma City, Oklahoma 73105
(405) 521-2502 ext. 61

OREGON
Oregon State Archives
800 Summer Street, NE
Salem, Oregon 97310
(503) 373-0701

PENNSYLVANIA
Pennsylvania State Archives
3rd and Forester Streets
Harrisburg, Pennsylvania
 17108-1026
(717) 783-3281

RHODE ISLAND
Rhode Island State Archives
337 Westminster Street
Providence, Rhode Island 02903
(401) 277-2353

SOUTH CAROLINA
South Carolina Department
 of Archives and History
Attention: Reference Service
P.O. Box 11669
Columbia, South Carolina 29211
(803) 734-8577

SOUTH DAKOTA
South Dakota State Archives
900 Governor's Drive
Pierre, South Dakota 57501-2217
(605) 773-3804

TENNESSEE
Public Service Section
Tennessee State Library
 and Archives
403 7th Avenue North
Nashville, Tennessee 37243-0312
(615) 741-2561

TEXAS
Texas State Library
Archives Division
P.O. Box 12927
Austin, Texas 78711
(512) 463-5480

UTAH
Family History Library
35 North, West Temple Street
Salt Lake City, Utah 84150
(801) 240-2331

VERMONT
General Services Center
 Reference/Research Section
Drawer 33
Montpelier, Vermont 05633-7601
(802) 828-3286

VIRGINIA
Virginia State Library
Archives Branch
11th and Capitol Square
Richmond, Virginia 23219
(804) 786-2306

WASHINGTON
Office of the Secretary of State
Division of Archives and
  Records Management
P.O. Box 40238
Olympia, Washington 98504-0238
(206) 753-5485

WEST VIRGINIA
West Virginia Department
  of Culture and History
Archives and History Division
The Cultural Center
1900 Kanawha Boulevard East
Charleston, West Virginia
  25305-0300
(304) 558-0220

WISCONSIN
Archives Division of the State
  Historical Society of Wisconsin
816 State Street
Madison, Wisconsin 53706
(608) 264-6460

WYOMING
Wyoming State Archives
Barrett Building
Cheyenne, Wyoming 82002
(307) 777-7826

The OR and
the ORN

IF YOU CONSIDER YOUR SEARCH for a Civil War ancestor complete once your letters have exhausted the information in the state and national archives, you are in for a very happy surprise. What may be one of the most exciting and rewarding parts of your search lies ahead of you. You must face the fact that, extremely valuable and indispensable as the state and national personnel records are, most of them are quite brief, completely impersonal, and as mechanical as a robot's diary: enlisted, promoted, absent on leave, sick, discharged, captured, pensioned, died.

There are thousands upon thousands of records, both official and unofficial, that are not found in a soldier's personnel file. These records vary from the precise and detailed battle reports and correspondence of the *Official Records* to the vivid and compelling stories of soldiers as found in diaries, personal narratives, and the histories of the regiments in which they served. By far the most important set of books in print is the huge 128-volume *Official Records of the Union and Confederate Armies in the War of the Rebellion,* popularly called the *OR* by Civil War scholars. In 1864 the United States government began collecting all the available Union armies' records, reports, orders, and memorandums ever issued,

posted, filed, or printed. After the war the federal government collected all the similar Confederate records. By 1881 Washington had begun the tremendous job of printing the more important of these records. Nineteen years later, the job was complete—128 volumes containing over 138,000 pages of records.

A companion set is the *Official Records of the Union and Confederate Navies in the War of the Rebellion,* or the *ORN.* Begun in 1894, the series took twenty-eight years to complete in thirty-one volumes. These two sets, the *OR* and the *ORN,* together with an accompanying atlas, famous for its accuracy and size, make up the most used and quoted set of Civil War records in existence. This is due to their reliability, vast coverage, and availability. Most large city libraries, all state universities, and many smaller colleges have both the *OR* and the *ORN,* and they are there for anyone to use. These records have also been duplicated on microfilm. Both the *OR* and the *ORN* have been reprinted jointly by and can be obtained from Morningside Bookshop, P.O. Box 1087, Dayton, Ohio 45401 (513-461-6736); Broadfoot Publishing Company, 1907 Buena Vista Circle, Wilmington, North Carolina 28405 (910-686-4816); and the National Historical Society, P.O. Box 8200, Harrisburg, Pennsylvania 17105. Microfilm of the *OR* and the *ORN* is available from the National Archives. If you have space for a set of the *OR,* the reprint is much more satisfactory to use than the microfilm. Available only from Broadfoot is a fine (*Supplement to the Official Records,* a huge, fifty-volume edition that includes reports not located, misplaced Union and Confederate reports, relevant correspondence, itineraries of the units, records of the secret service, and much more. It should also be noted that Morningside, while heavily into the reprint business, has by far the largest number of Civil War books available anywhere in the United States. Free catalogs from both Morningside and Broadfoot will open a vast new Civil War book world to you.

In any Civil War research the *OR* and the *ORN* are really indispensable. They give firsthand reports written by ships' captains, regimental colonels, and brigade commanders who directed and took part in the great land battles and naval engagements of the war. If great-grandfather's regiment was in any noteworthy fighting, there is a good chance that

what he saw will be retold by other men who were there, if not by great-grandfather himself. The story may be a bit biased, for in many cases an officer's report was a defense of his own actions. Most of the time, however, it will be close to the truth as he saw it and perhaps as great-grandfather fought it. The chances of your relatives' name being specifically mentioned in the *OR* or the *ORN* will depend upon his rank. This is because enlisted men did the fighting, not the organizing, directing, and reporting of the fighting. That was the officers' job. Generals are frequently mentioned, and their reports are often printed. You can shake thousands of colonels and hundreds of navy captains out of the *OR* and the *ORN*. As the rank decreases, an officer's chance of survival in print decreases.

It is remarkable, though, just how many men of lower ranks and grades are mentioned by name. It is this fact that gives the single 1,242-page *OR* index and the smaller 475-page *ORN* index a special significance. If you know only great-grandfather's name and not the state in which he enlisted or the regiment in which he fought, or if the Civil War soldier's letter you possess has no identification other than a signature, there is a fair chance of associating that name with a regiment, ship, or state. Just look up the name in the *OR* or the *ORN* index.

These two indexes are extremely useful, but there is a small trick in learning how to use them. Suppose you find a letter signed by Paul J. Semmes. In the *OR* index you will find, listed after his name, I, 11, 12, 19, 21, 25, 27, 29, 51; III, l; IV, 1. The 128 *OR* books are divided into four parts, called series. They are I, II, III, and IV. So the I, III, and IV indicate that references to Semmes will be found in Series, I, III, and IV. The numbers after the Roman numerals are volume numbers, not page numbers. I, 11 means that in Series I and in volume eleven's own separate index in the back of the book you will find the name, Paul J. Semmes, and the pages in that particular volume where he is mentioned. Be sure to note that the general index has a section on additions and corrections.

In 1968 the National Archives published *Military Operations of the Civil War. A Guide-Index to the Official Records of the Union and Confederate Armies, 1861–1865.* This resource is now out of print but is soon to be republished. This index, although not absolutely necessary to the

"soldier hunter," has its uses. You may wish information on the battle of Malvern Hill, Virginia. In Volume II, section L, page 39, you will find (1) a reference to the pages in *The Official Atlas of the Civil War* on which maps of Malvern Hill appear; (2) a listing of volumes and pages that contain the official reports of all military action in the area; (3) Union reports by various officers; (4) Confederate reports by various officers; (5) any Union and Confederate correspondence mentioning the area. The *Index* lists all the entries concerning this battle within the space of less than half a page. It would take a trained professional historian many days to search out all these references without the aid of the *Guide-Index*. When this valuable resource is republished, you will be able to order it from the National Archives Publications Service Branch, 8th and Pennsylvania Avenue, NW, Washington, D. C. 20408.

The Official Atlas of the Civil War is an unexcelled volume as important as it is large. It weighs over ten pounds, and measures over sixteen inches tall and thirteen inches wide. It has over 400 pages of maps and engravings, which include 821 maps and 209 drawings, all done during or just after the Civil War. The maps cover many, but not all, of the major campaigns and many smaller battles. Published by the government to accompany the *Official Records*, it is worth every penny of what you will pay for it, given its size and contents. You can get it quickly from Broadfoot or Morningside or with a bit more time from most bookstores.

A very fine smaller book of maps is Francis H. Kennedy's *Civil War Battlefield Guide*. This fine atlas, not large or expensive, contains many modern topographical maps of areas over which the Civil War battles were fought. These modern maps then are overlaid with the exact locations of trenches, etc. They are so accurate as to enable the modern historian or Civil War enthusiast to pinpoint any battlefield location on any map in the atlas. You may perhaps be able to determine the vicinity where a Confederate trench ran through your garden or pasture or front yard. This atlas is the first of its kind for modern locations. It may be obtained through bookstores or by writing Conservation Fund, 17800 North Kent Street, Suite 1120, Arlington, Virginia 22209.

Massive and comprehensive as the 160 volumes of the *OR* and the

ORN appear, they are still only the small visible part of the giant iceberg of historical nonpersonal documents, the great bulk of which is hidden unpublished under the surface in the National Archives in Washington. The nonpersonal military records are a little more inaccessible than is the information in great-grandfather's military service record jacket or in his pension file. These millions of documents contain every conceivable type of military information and are concerned with everything from one-man details to one-hundred-thousand-man armies, and from naval buoys to naval stations and battleships. Naturally, the vast Union forces are covered more thoroughly than those of the Confederacy. Even at that, the federal government is the chief repository for most Confederate records. You can travel pretty far into these records with writing paper and checkbook. Here you will not be searching directly for great-grandfather, but for his regiment and his battles, or his ship and his cruise.

Let's suppose that your relative was a sailor. Suppose also that you have exhausted his personnel folder and his pension and medical records and that you have squeezed your local library's *ORN* for every scrap of information concerning his ship, the Union ironclad, *Keokuk,* sunk in Charleston Harbor in April 1863. Next, you would send a letter requesting further information to the Military Reference Branch (NNRM), National Archives and Records Administration, General Reference Branch (NNRG-P), 7th and Pennsylvania Avenue, NW, Washington, D.C. 20408 (202-501-5170). (This address is one of the most important in this whole book. If you are doing in-depth research, it is one of the principal doors to experts.) The reply would inform you that a copy of a muster roll of the *Keokuk* was available for sale and three rolls of microfilm concerning the ship, as well. You would also be told that the archives have for sale a 500-page *List of Logbooks of the U.S. Navy, Stations and Miscellaneous Units, 1801–1947* (Special List 44). Any of these logs can be bought on microfilm. With such a log, you could follow your sailor's travels through chase and blockade, day by day. Fortunately, you do not need to own a microfilm reader, even though they are becoming fairly inexpensive. Most libraries of even moderate size own at least one microfilm reader, and it is a rare librarian who will refuse you the use of one.

Continuing with your navy search, you could write or, better, phone

the Navy Historical Center, Washington Navy Yard, Washington, D.C. 20374 (202-433-4131). It has a large collection of navy documents, as well as one of the best collections of navy pictures and photographs in existence, and it will duplicate any of them for you for a nominal fee. I might add that it has a file on every navy officer from the beginning of to well into this century. Alas, it did not pay such attention to the common sailor, so the enlisted man will be, as always, more of a problem. A set of books that is very useful for tracking a ship's history is that great, eight-volume set sold by the National Archives entitled *Dictionary of American Naval Fighting Ships.* These volumes give a short history of every fighting ship in the navy from the American Revolution to the present, including Confederate ships of the Civil War period. No other reference contains this information in one set of books.

It may be that you will have to search the National Archives beyond the end of the war in 1865. This is because many Civil War veterans served on beyond the end of the war in regular United States Army regiments or aboard United States Navy ships and stations. The National Archives Personnel Records are limited mainly to the following years:

United States Army	1775-1912
United States Navy	1776-1885
United States Marines	1798-1895

For personnel records beyond these dates you should write to the army or navy personnel departments, Washington, D.C.

One unusual example of service after the Civil War was that of General Joe Wheeler. Wheeler was a major general of Confederate cavalry. At the end of the war he was imprisoned with ex-President Jefferson Davis as a dangerous enemy leader whom many wanted hanged. Any type of reasoning would come to the conclusion that Wheeler's military career had come to a complete and disastrous end. Thirty-three years later Confederate General Wheeler was Major General Wheeler, United States Army, directing American troops as they charged up the slopes of a hill near Santiago, Cuba, in the Spanish-American War. The story goes that, when the Spanish line broke and ran before his advancing regiments, he forgot

time and place and shouted after his charging troopers, "After 'em boys! We've got the Yankees on the run!"

Any number of Union men remained in the Federal army after the war. There were even Confederate prisoners who joined the Union Army during the war. They joined, not as deserters or turncoats but as Indian fighters, and were labeled "Galvanized Yankees," the idea being that just as a sheet of galvanized iron is covered with a thin layer of zinc, so the ex-Confederate was galvanized with a thin layer of "official Yankee," blue coat and all. Underneath, however, lay a hardcore Rebel. Some of these "Galvanized Yankees" remained in the army after the war.

This all goes to point up the fact that your veteran may have had a service career after the end of the great Civil War, and he may even have served on both sides. Such service would be indicated through a pension file record or a notation of enlistment in the regular United States Army found in the soldier's personnel file. The Navy, especially, grew in size after the war, and a good many Civil War bluejackets' records extend on toward the turn of the century. Before leaving this chapter, I should mention what were, during the war, the two most important government publications of all. They told your soldier when to get up, when and how to drill, eat, work, and generally disrupt what had been a peaceful life. And they granted his officers an authority that usually added to the enlisted man's misery for the duration of his stay in the service. By now you have surely guessed the titles—*Regulations for the Army of the Confederate States* and *Revised Regulations for the Army of the United States.* Both are available from the National Historical Society, P.O. Box 8200, Harrisburg, Pennsylvania 17105, and provide fascinating and informative reading.

Your Guide
to Millions of Pages

THERE IS YET MORE BEYOND the *OR*, the *ORN*, the giant miscellaneous holdings of the National Archives, and the holdings of the various states. There are books, rosters, and regimental histories by the tens of thousands. For these one must turn to the library. Here, in public and private collections across the country, are deposited books, articles, memoirs, diaries, and journals on the war. The library at your state capital or larger university will often be your best help. If you are too far from either of these, your hometown library will do. A library can borrow books from any part of the nation through a system called "Interlibrary Loan."

Your first concern will be to find a really good guide to the endless amount of Civil War literature scattered across the United States. The books that will be your guides to these new sources are known as bibliographies. They contain lists of Civil War publications by subject, title, and author. Since 1865 quite a few of these bibliographies have been published. There are, however, two guides on the market today that have no equal. The first is *Civil War Books: A Critical Bibliography,* by Allan Nevins, James I. Robertson, Jr., and Bell I. Wiley. It is in two volumes

Davenport, Alfred.
Camp and field life of the Fifth New York voluntee: infantry. (Duryee zouaves.) By Alfred Davenport New York, Dick and Fitzgerald, 1879.

485 p front (port.) pl 19½ᵐ.

This thoroughly useful narrative, based on diaries and letters, covers admirably the exploits of a regiment that saw valiant service through Chancellorsville.

Davidson, Henry M   *d.* 1900.
History of Battery A. First regiment of Ohio vol. light artillery. Milwaukee. Daily Wisconsin steam printing house, 1865.

vii, ¡9¡–199 p. 19½ᵐ.

A cursory, early account, based largely on company records, alleged diaries, and the author's own recollections.

Davis, Charles E   *b.* 1842 *or* 1843–1915.
Three years in the army. The story of the Thirteenth Massachusetts volunteers from July 16, 1861, to August 1, 1864. By Charles E. Davis, jr. Boston, Estes and Lauriat, 1894.

xxxv, 476 p. maps. 23½ cm.

Five diaries and numerous official sources formed the basis for this highly regarded history of a unit that served in the Army of the Potomac until its disbandment in the summer of 1864.

Davis, Nicholas A
The campaign from Texas to Maryland. By Rev. Nicholas A. Davis ... Richmond. Printed at the office of the Presbyterian committee of publication of the Confederate States. 1863.

165, ¡1¡ p. 2 port. (incl. front.) 19½ᵐ.

One of the better narratives treating of Hood's Texas Brigade; contains personal comments on almost all aspects of the war.

Davis, Nicholas A
Chaplain Davis and Hood's Texas Brigade. Edited and with an introd. by Donald E. Everett. San Antonio, Principia Press of Trinity University, 1962.

234 p. 24 cm.

A vastly expanded version, with good editorial trappings added, of Davis's *Campaign from Texas* . . .

Davis, Oliver Wilson
Life of David Bell Birney, majo. general United States volunteers. Philadelphia, King & Baird; New York, Sheldon & co., 1867.

xii, 418 p. front. (port.) 26ᵐ

Its eulogistic passages notwithstanding, this military biography is a basic source for any study of the Army of the Potomac.

Davis, William Watts Hart, 1820–1910.
History of the 104th Pennsylvania regiment, from August 22nd, 1861, to September 30th, 1864. By W. W. H. Davis ... Philadelphia, J. B. Rogers, printer, 1866.

vii p., 1 l., 9–364 p. incl. front. pl., port. 23 cm.

Col. Davis entered the Civil War with the intention of writing his unit's history, and the resulting study is a highly reliable commentary on the Peninsular and Carolina coastal campaigns.

Dawes, Rufus R 1838–1899.
Service with the Sixth Wisconsin volunteers. By Rufus R. Dawes ... Marietta, O., E. R. Alderman & sons, 1890.

2 p. l., v, ¡5¡–330 p. front., illus., port. 22½ᵐ.

The best narrative by a soldier from the Midwest; based on the author's letters and diary, the work is a standard source for the Eastern battles and the Iron Brigade.

Dawes, Rufus R 1838–1899.
Service with the Sixth Wisconsin Volunteers. Edited with an introd. by Alan T. Nolan. Madison, State Historical Society of Wisconsin for Wisconsin Civil War Centennial Commission, 1962.

xv, 330 (i. e. 336) p. illus., ports. 23 cm.

A needed reissue of the original, with a revealing introduction and critical bibliography.

Dawson, Francis W
Reminiscences of Confederate service, 1861–1865. By Capt. Francis W. Dawson ... Charleston, S. C., The News and courier book presses, 1882.

180 p. 23½ᵐ.

Dawson was an Englishman who served on Longstreet's staff and afterwards became the internationally known editor of the Charleston *Courier*; a penetrating commentary, deserving of republication.

A page from *Civil War Books*, by Nevins, Robertson, and Wiley. This is one of the most important library guides you will use in your search of regimental history.

and is published by the Louisiana State University Press. These two volumes list almost all the significant as well as many of the insignificant Civil War books printed from the 1850s to the 1960s. They give a brief statement about the contents of each book and also contain helpful comments about the book's accuracy and completeness. Let us suppose that in your research you are referred to Rufus R. Dawes' *Service with the Sixth Wisconsin Volunteers.* A quick look in "Nevins, Robertson, and Wiley" will tell you that this book is "the best narrative by a soldier from the Midwest; based on the author's letters and diary, the work is a standard source for the Eastern battles and the Iron Brigade." Suppose another one of your references is a pamphlet by William H. Clark entitled "Reminiscences of the Thirty-fourth Regiment, Massachusetts Volunteer Infantry." *Civil War Books* will tell you that this work is "little more than a footnote on the 1864 battle of New Market, Va." Such comments will help you decide whether you want to get a work through interlibrary loan, and they may save you from buying the book sight unseen and being disappointed when you receive it. *Civil War Books* is available in most libraries and can be purchased from Morningside Bookshop and Broadfoot Publishing Company, to name a few. If you want to buy a Civil War book not currently included on a publisher's list, or if you have inherited some Civil War books that you want to evaluate, Broadfoot Publishing Company has published *Civil War Books: A Priced Checklist,* which enables you to put a price on almost any Civil War book. This title can be purchased from Broadfoot Publishing Company.

The second and by far the most complete guide to regimental publications and personal narratives is Charles E. Dornbusch's *Military Bibliography of the Civil War,* in four volumes. They are published by the New York Public Library, Fifth Avenue and 42nd Street, New York, N.Y. 10018. This set is also available by sending your order to Hope Farm Press and Book Shop, 1708 Route 212, Saugerties, New York, New York 12477 (914-679-6809). This volume lists practically every book ever written about military units, both Northern and Southern, and includes, as well, most of the articles concerned with regimental histories that are to be found in journals and in the leading professional history magazines. It is an invaluable work. It is not expensive and can be obtained or ordered in any bookstore. Suppose you know of an ancestor who was in the

5TH CAVALRY

Mustered in: January 9 to May 5, 1864.
Mustered out: October 31, 1865.
Mass soldiers VI 492–544.
Mass in the war 781–3.

Bowditch, Charles Pickering
War letters of Charles P. Bowditch. *Massachusetts historical society proceedings* LVII (1923/24) 414–95. facs., plate (port.).   73

1st Battalion of Cavalry

Mustered in and attached to 26th regiment of New York cavalry: December 30, 1864 to January 2, 1865.
Mustered out: June 30, 1865.
Mass soldiers VI 545–65.
Mass in the war 784.

INFANTRY

1ST INFANTRY

Mustered in: May 23–27, 1861.
Mustered out: May 25, 1864.
Mass soldiers I 1–68.
Mass in the war 99–112.

Constitution, by laws, and rules of order of the First regiment relief association, organized, June 15, 1863. Boston, J. E. Farwell & co., printers, 1863. 9, (1) p. 14cm.   MHi   74

First regiment Massachusetts volunteer infantry veteran association. Boston, Mass., February, 1911. Fiftieth anniversary roster [Boston, 1911] [32] p. port. 23½cm.   DLC   75
Caption title.

First regiment of infantry Massachusetts volunteer militia, Colonel Robert Cowdin, commanding. In service of the United States, in answer to the President's first call for troops to suppress the rebellion, April 5, 1861. Compiled from original papers in the Adjutant general and Auditor's offices of the Commonwealth. Boston, Wright and Potter print co., 1903. 50 p. 2 plates (facs., port.). 24cm.
        DLC NN   76
Unit roster [15]–50. On cover: 1st regiment infantry M.V.M., 1861. "Introduction" signed: Luke Edward Jenkins, Private Company B.

Memorial service in memory of the dead of the First regt. Massachusetts volunteer infantry, 1861–64, Faneuil hall, Boston, Mass., May 21, 1911. [16] p. 23cm.   DLC NN   77
Title from cover which includes the program. A roster of those killed in action and those who have died since the war.

Bardeen, Charles William, 1847–1924.
A little fifer's war diary, by C. W. Bardeen, formerly of Co. D., 1st Mass. vol. inf. With an introduction by Nicholas Murray Butler. Syracuse, N. Y., C. W. Bardeen, 1910. 329 p. illus., maps, ports. 24cm.   NN   78
Facsimile of the author's discharge printed on inside of back cover.

Cowdin, Robert, 1806?–1874.
Gen. Cowdin and the First Massachusetts regiment of volunteers. Boston, J. E. Farwell and co., printers, 1864. 19 p. 23cm.
        DLC M MHi   79

Cudworth, Warren Handel, 1825–1883.
History of the First regiment (Massachusetts infantry), from the 25th of May, 1861, to the 25th of May, 1864, including brief references to the operations of the Army of the Potomac, by Warren H. Cudworth, Chaplain of the Regiment. . . . Boston, Walker, Fuller and co., 1866. 528 p. plates (illus.). 20cm.   DLC NN   80
Unit roster [498]–528. Coulter 103.

Cutler, Frederick Morse, 1874–
The old First Massachusetts coast artillery in war and peace, by Frederick Morse Cutler. Boston, Pilgrim press [1917] 180 p. plates (illus., ports.). 19½cm.   NN   81
Civil war 46–79.

Darling, Charles B
Historical sketch of the First regiment infantry, Massachusetts volunteer militia, compiled by Chas. B. Darling. Boston. [Alfred Mudge & Sons, printers] 1890. [40] p. illus., ports. 27½ × 35½cm.   DLC   82
Advertising matter included. On cover: Souvenir of the dedication of the new armory, June, 1890.

Frye, James A   1863–1933.
The First regiment of heavy artillery, 1844–1899. In Regiments and armories of Massachusetts, edited by Charles W. Hall, 1899 I 338–60.   83
Civil war, 344–52.

Holden, Leverett Dana, 1843–1932.
My first and last fights, delivered before the Malden club, Feb. 5, 1914. Fredericksburg to Gettysburg. Memories of the Civil war, by Leverett D. Holden. Malden, Samuel Tilden, printer [1914] 85 p. front. (port.). 16½cm.   NN   84

Kingsbury, Allen Alonzo, 1840–1862.
The hero of Medfield, containing the journals and letters of Allen Alonzo Kingsbury, of Medfield, member of Co. H, Chelsea volunteers, Mass. 1st reg., who was killed by the Rebels near Yorktown, April 26, 1862. Also, notice of the other three soldiers belonging to the same company and killed at the same time,

Here is an example from Charles E. Dornbusch's well-known *Military Bibliography of the Civil War*. This is the most important single work in print today for those searching a regiment's complete history. Note National Union Catalog symbols after each item, which aid in locating each book or article.

...section, autobiographical works are listed first under ...graphical works follow under heading I.

...LDEN, 1831–1893.
...den Auchmuty, Fifth
...ac. Edited by E.S.A.
Privately printed. [n.p., 189–] 127 p. 20cm.
                                 NHi *1842*
NHi's copy has presentation inscription of Jan. 1895. The editor is probably the wife, Ellen Schermerhorn Auchmuty, 1837–1927.

BACON, CYRUS, 1836?–1868.
A Michigan surgeon at Chancellorsville one hundred years ago. Edited by Frank Whitehouse, Jr. and Walter M. Whitehouse. *University of Michigan medical bulletin* xxix (1963) 315–31.   *1843*

BAER, GEORGE FREDERICK, 1842–1911.
Oration of George F. Baer at the unveiling of the soldiers and sailors' monument at Allentown, Penna., October 19, 1899. 8 p. 27½cm.
    Title from cover.   CSmH *1844*

BALL, LEVI CHANDLER, 1809–1875.
Speech on the war, by Major L. Chandler Ball, delivered at Hoosick Falls, December 9th, 1863. Washington, D. C., Chronicle print, 1893. 24 p. 23cm.   DLC NB *1845*

BANKS, NATHANIEL PRENTISS, 1816–1894.
An address delivered by Maj. General N. P. Banks at the Customhouse, New Orleans, on the Fourth of July, 1865. 8 p. 22cm.
                          CSmH *1846*

I

Celebration of the centennial of the birth of General Nathaniel Prentice Banks, Waltham, Massachusetts, January 30, 1916. [Waltham, Waltham pub. co., printers, 1916] 31 p. front. (port.). 23cm.   DNW *1847*

Department of the Gulf. Historical sketch of Major Gen. N. P. Banks' civil and military administration in Louisiana. Tenth edition. New York, 1864. 12 p. 20cm.   CSmH *1848*
   Text signed: P. W.

General Banks. *Illinois central magazine* ii 1 (July 1913) 13–22, ii 2 (August 1913) 13–18. facsim., 2 illus., port.   *1849*

Harrington, Fred Harvey, 1912–
  . . . Fighting politician, Major General N. P. Banks, by Fred Harvey Harrington. Philadelphia, University of Pennsylvania

press, 1948. xi, (1), 301 p. front. (port.). 23cm.   NN *1849A*
  At head of title: The American historical association.
  "Theater of operations of Major General N. P. Banks, 1861–1862 [1863–1865"] maps, end papers.

BARLOW, FRANCIS CHANNING, 1834–1896.

I

In memoriam Francis Channing Barlow, 1834–1896. Published by the authority of the State of New York under the supervision of the New York monuments commission. Albany, J. B. Lyon co., printers, 1923. front. (port.), plates (illus., maps, ports.). 27½cm. NHi *1850*
  On cover: Major-General Francis C. Barlow at Gettysburg and other battlefields.

BARLOW, JOHN WHITNEY, 1938–1914.
Personal reminiscences of the war, by Lieut. Col. John W. Barlow. *MOLLUS-Wis* i 106–19.
                                1851

BARNUM, HENRY ALANSON, 1833–1892.
Oration delivered by Major-General Henry A. Barnum, before the Society of the Army of the Cumberland at Detroit, Nov. 15, 1871. New York, E. S. Dodge & co., printers, 1871. 21 p. 23cm.   DLC *1852*

BARTLETT, WILLIAM FRANCIS, 1840–1876.

I

A record of the dedication of the statue of Major General Francis Bartlett, a tribute of the Commonwealth of Massachusetts, May 27, 1904. Boston, Printed by Wright and Potter print. co., 1905. 82 p. plates (ports.). 24½cm.
                           NN *1853*
  The Council "ordered, that Francis Hurtubis, Jr., private secretary·to the Governor, be authorized to edit and publish a report of the proceedings."

BAYARD, GEORGE DASHIEL, 1835–1862.

I

Bayard, Samuel John,   –1879.
  The life of George Dashiell Bayard . . . by Samuel J. Bayard. New York, G. P. Putnam's Sons, 1874. ix, [11]–337 p. front. (port.), 2 plates (illus., fold. map). 19½cm.
                       CSmH *1854*

BELL, LUTHER V., 1806–1862.

I

Ellis, George Edward, 1814–1894.
  Memoir of Luther V. Bell, prepared by vote of the Massachusetts historical society, by

C. E. Dornbusch's very important work not only lists all material relating to regimental histories, both North and South, but gives you page after page of personal narrative, memoirs, and diaries, as well.

Twenty-first Ohio Infantry. Dornbusch lists each of Ohio's regiments of cavalry, artillery, and infantry. He then proceeds to list everything that has been written concerning each of Ohio's military units. You will find in Dornbusch that there are one published diary, one complete history, and two articles written about the Twenty-first Ohio. If it is the Seventeenth Virginia Infantry that you are interested in, you will find that there have been two books, one history and roster, two orations, and two articles concerning the Seventeenth. You will also find that the Nineteenth Pennsylvania Cavalry had practically nothing written about it, nor did the Third North Carolina Artillery. Volume I of Dornbusch covers the southern, border, and western states and the United States Territories. Volume II covers the northern states. Volume III is especially useful in obtaining the stories of specific state military units as they fought at Gettysburg, Shiloh, and the like. Volume IV is an update of Volumes I-III. In publishing his book Dornbusch not only has made it possible for anyone to search out every scrap of existing literature concerning his ancestor's regiment but has done an inestimable service to collectors of antique arms and equipment by making Civil War histories so easy to locate.

There is one little trick to getting the most out of Dornbusch. At the very end of each bibliographic entry you will find a series of capital and small letters, such as NHi, CT, TCU, RR. These are National Union Catalog symbols and refer to the particular library where these books and articles may be found. NHi is the abbreviation for New York Historical Society, CT stands for Connecticut State Library, Hartford, Connecticut, and TCU stands for the University of Chattanooga's library. Suppose you have found listed a history of the Twenty-fourth Massachusetts. The Twenty-fourth Massachusetts has after it the letters DLC and NN. DLC and NN indicate that a copy of this regimental history may be found in the Library of Congress (DLC) and in the New York Public Library (NN). Most librarians have reference books that can interpret these signs for you and will be glad to help you in your interlibrary loan hunt. Every regimental history and regimental narrative cited in Dornbusch has been published on microfiche and is available for sale in a huge series by University Publications of America, 4520 East-West Highway, Bethesda, Maryland 20814-3389.

Mention should be made here of the works of two other authors that go hand in hand with Dornbusch. Suppose all you knew of great-grand-father was that he belonged to some Confederate outfit known as the "Flat Rock Rifles," or perhaps the "Pee Dee Wild Cats." In a two-volume work by William Amann entitled *Personnel of the Civil War* you will find that the "Flat Rock Rifles" were Company C, Twentieth Virginia Infantry, and that the "Pee Dee Wild Cats" were Company K, Twenty-sixth North Carolina Infantry. A sampling of names will indicate just how useful Amann's book can be: "Fishing Creek Avengers," Company D, Twenty-sixth Mississippi Infantry; "Orphan Brigade," First Kentucky Brigade; "Haw River Boys," Company D, Thirty-fifth North Carolina; "Stars of Equality," Company E, Nineteenth Louisiana Infantry; "Rattlesnake Rangers," Company C, Nineteenth Battalion, Georgia Cavalry; "Bartow Yankee Killers," Company A, Twenty-third Georgia Infantry.

Many of the Northern troops went by similar names, such as "Richland County Plow Boys," Company D, Eleventh Wisconsin Infantry; "Jayhawkers," Company I, Ninth Kansas Regular Cavalry; "Volcano Blues," Company D, California Fourth Regular Infantry; "Mason's Invincibles," Company B, Eighteenth Massachusetts Regular Infantry; and "Guppy Guards," Company D, Twenty-third Wisconsin Infantry.

Thomas Yoseloff published Amann's book as well as a similar single volume by William Tancig entitled *Confederate Military Land Units.* Both are out of print but available in larger libraries. On request, the National Archives will also supply you with the same type of information that Amann and Tancig provide.

What *Military Bibliography of the Civil War* and *Civil War Books* are to the armies of that great war, *American Civil War Navies,* by Myron J. Smith, Jr., is to the Northern and Southern sea services. Published in 1972 by Scarecrow Press, Inc., Box 656, Metuchen, New Jersey 08840, it is a fine one-volume bibliographic listing of almost every English language book, article, or paper of any significance published from the 1850s to 1972. There are over 2,800 entries. If you wish to add to the material you have obtained from the state or national archives or from the *ORN,* you should get a copy of this book.

A regimental history will trace a particular regiment from its mustering-in ceremony through all its battles to the final disbanding of the

survivors. The histories vary tremendously in quality and usefulness. With a few rare exceptions, every regiment in both great armies, North and South, has had something of its history recorded. It may be only a few pages, as in the case of the forgotten Eightieth Illinois Infantry and the Twenty-fourth South Carolina, or it may be an extensive literature in books and magazines, as in the case of Louisiana's famous Washington Artillery or the Twentieth Maine Infantry that stepped through the gates of everlasting glory at Gettysburg.

Regimental histories are especially good for tracing the higher ranking officers—the majors, lieutenant colonels, and colonels. Almost all these histories give detailed biographies of these officers, and many include anecdotes and much personal information gathered by fellow officers and comrades at the time. More often than not these books include photographs of all the higher ranking officers in the regiment, making the regimental history a really indispensable source for searchers of these leaders.

A few years ago I purchased a photograph of a serene-looking much-bewhiskered Civil War officer. Signed in black ink with a firm hand across the bottom was "Col. Cilley, 1st Me. Cav." When I got home, I headed straight for my library and pulled from the shelf Dornbusch's volume containing Maine regimental histories. Here I found a searcher's dream come true. There were twenty-five separate entries, including a 735-page regimental history that contained a photograph and much information on Cilley. In addition to a second 436-page history, there were two articles written by the Colonel himself, as well as many other articles. Quite a few of the articles related to Cilley, his bravery, and his leadership.

A few months after acquiring the Cilley photograph I was able to obtain a personally autographed photograph of Confederate cavalry leader John Hunt Morgan. It was Morgan who, in July 1863, led 2,500 grey-clad cavalrymen in a magnificent sweep into Kentucky, Indiana, and Ohio, only to be captured with his whole command. Morgan escaped from the Ohio penitentiary at Columbus where he and his officers were kept. He returned south to become one of the best-known and most dashing of all Confederate cavalry leaders until his death in September 1864, near Greeneville, Tennessee.

In looking into the lives of better-known officers such as Morgan, you

Above are the photographs of the famous Confederate cavalry general, John Hunt Morgan, who invaded southern Ohio with a large force of cavalry, and lesser-known Colonel Jonathan P. Cilley, of the First Maine Cavalry, often wounded in battle and once near death. As is the case North or South, there was much information on these two men for they were officers above the rank of major. Collectors don't take much of a gamble here, for they can be reasonably certain to find more than a little information.

may go again to Dornbusch, who also lists biographies. Nevins, Robertson, and Wiley's *Civil War Books* will do just fine, also, in giving you a list of books to work on. Again, remember that, although Nevins, Robertson, and Wiley's *Civil War Books* parallels Dornbusch, the latter has a more complete listing and includes sources other than books. *Civil War Books*, however, has a special quality, for it gives a short critical evaluation of each of its entries, which Dornbusch does not. So take your pick. They are the best there are in their field.

Another useful book is Frederick Dyer's three-volume *A Compendium of the War of the Rebellion*. Frederick Dyer, a Connecticut drummer boy, was immensely proud of being a Northern veteran in the War of the Rebellion. He was so fiercely proud that he made it a personal obligation

to write and commit to memory the histories of over 2,000 Union regiments formed between 1861 and 1865. Needless to say, Dyer was an intellectual oddity and was looked upon with wonder and amazement by fellow veterans.

In 1903, at the urging of his comrades, fifty-four-year-old Dyer began the truly awe-inspiring task of outlining the histories, commanders, and movements of all the regiments in the Union army. Working constantly and alone, he finished his work five years later and called it *A Compendium of the War of the Rebellion*. Dyer's work was reproduced in 1959 in three volumes by T. Y. Yoseloff. Morningside and Broadfoot have both reprinted Dyer's *Compendium* recently.

Fortunately for those with Southern ancestors, there is now a marvelous multivolume set giving the histories of every Confederate state unit— a Confederate Dyer's at long last! This set was created by Stewart Sifakis and is entitled *A Compendium of the Confederate Armies.* This great work is published by Facts on File, 460 Park Avenue South, New York, New York 10016 (212-683-2244). As of 1994, the eleven-volume work included separate volumes for Alabama, Louisiana, Mississippi, North Carolina, Tennessee, Texas, and Virginia; a pair of two-in-one volumes, one covering Florida and Arkansas and the other covering South Carolina and Georgia; one volume covering Kentucky, Maryland, Missouri, and the Indian units; and a volume on tables of organization.

A very early (1899) set of books related to Confederate state units is the multivolume *Confederate Military History,* first edited by General C. A. Evans of Georgia. Morningside Press has reprinted this classic, as has Broadfoot Publishing Company. The Broadfoot expanded edition, with ten times as many biographical sketches as the original edition, contains nineteen volumes, including a new two-volume index.

These volumes vary in quality, for the state histories were written by different notable Confederates of varying historical competence and talent. Some of the histories, such as that of Florida, are well organized. Texas, on the other hand, is spotty and poorly done. At any rate, they may be of some help to you. For a starter, you should go to the Index. As mentioned before, the greatest virtue of these books is that they are available almost anywhere in the United States, and they do cover many Southern regiments.

Most states that participated in the war also published their own official histories of each of their fighting units. Illinois has published eight volumes of regimental histories, *Report of the Adjutant General of the State of Illinois for the Years 1861–1866;* Massachusetts, *Massachusetts Soldiers, Sailors and Marines in the Civil War,* eight volumes; Florida, *Soldiers of Florida in the Seminole Indian, Civil and Spanish-American Wars,* one volume; New York, *New York in the War of the Rebellion, 1861– 1865,* six volumes. A list of the most useful regimental histories according to the leading authorities of each state will be found in Appendix B. Additions to this list can be found in Dornbusch's general references for each state.

If you cannot locate your regiment, use Dyer volumes 1 and 2 or the *OR* to see with whom your regiment was brigaded. It was a Civil War practice to band three to five regiments together into a brigade in which they fought as a unit. Thus the story of your brigade is essentially the story of your regiment. A trace of the other regiments in that brigade may lead directly to references to actions of your own regiment and enable you to begin putting the pieces together.

The biggest drawback to the state histories is usually their unavailability outside the individual states. Very few have been reprinted in modern times, and sometimes you cannot get them through interlibrary loan because they are too valuable to lend indiscriminately. You can have a distant library Xerox a particular regimental history. You may want to get an estimate of the cost for reproducing a page, for the total bill may run to more than you will want to pay for reproduction.

In addition to the official state regimental histories, which often are very brief, there are hundreds upon hundreds of single volumes devoted to one and only one regiment. The best of these will give you really splendid word pictures of marches, battle scenes, and descriptions of officers, messmates, and friends of your soldier, or of your soldier himself. In quite a few there are photographs of members of the regiment. Almost always there are a few pictures of the leading regimental officers and in many cases photographs of enlisted men. It is here that you may find a picture of great-grandfather or a photograph to go with your inscribed sword.

North Anna River May 23-26. Line of the Pamunkey May 26-28. Totopotomoy May 28-31. Cold Harbor June 1-12. Before Petersburg June 16-19. Siege of Petersburg June 16, 1864, to April 2, 1865. Jerusalem Plank Road June 22-23, 1864. Deep Bottom, north of the James, July 27-28. Mine Explosion, Petersburg, July 30 (Reserve). Demonstration north of the James August 13-20. Strawberry Plains, Deep Bottom, August 14-18. Ream's Station August 25. Boydton Plank Road, Hatcher's Run, October 27-28. Dabney's Mills February 5-7, 1865. Appomattox Campaign March 28-April 9. Boydton Road March 30-31. Fall of Petersburg April 2. Sailor's Creek April 6. High Bridge April 6-7. Farmville April 7. Appomattox C. H. April 9. Surrender of Lee and his army. At Burkesville April 11-May 2. March to Washington, D. C., May 2-15. Grand Review May 23. Mustered out May 31 and discharged June 7, 1865. Recruits transferred to 1st Maine Heavy Artillery.

Regiment lost during service 3 Officers and 189 Enlisted men killed and mortally wounded and 2 Officers and 182 Enlisted men by disease. Total 376.

20th REGIMENT INFANTRY.

Organized at Portland and mustered in August 29, 1862. Left State for Alexandria, Va., September 3. Attached to 1st Brigade, 1st Division, 5th Army Corps, Army Potomac, to October, 1862. 3rd Brigade, 1st Division, 5th Army Corps, to July, 1865.

SERVICE.—Battle of Antietam, Md., September 16-17, 1862. Shephardstown September 19. Advance to Falmouth, Va., October-November. Battle of Fredericksburg, Va., December 12-15. Expedition to Richards and Ellis Fords December 20-30. "Mud March" January 20-24, 1863. Chancellorsville Campaign April 27-May 6. Battle of Chancellorsville May 1-5. Gettysburg (Pa.) Campaign June 12-July 24. Aldie June 17. Upperville and Upperville June 21. Middleburg June 24. Battle of Gettysburg July 1-3. Pursuit of Lee to Manassas Gap, Va., July 5-24. Bristoe Campaign October 9-22. Advance to line of the Rappahannock November 7-8. Rappahannock Station November 7. Mine Run Campaign November 26-December 2. Campaign from the Rapidan to the James May 3-June 15, 1864. Battles of the Wilderness May 5-7. Laurel Hill May 8. Spottsylvania May 8-12. Spottsylvania C. H. May 12-21. North Anna River May 23-26. Jericho Mills May 23. Line of the Pamunkey May 26-28. Totopotomoy May 28-31. Cold Harbor June 1-3. Bethesda Church June 1-3. Before Petersburg June 16-19. Siege of Petersburg June 16, 1864, to April 2, 1865. Weldon Railroad June 21-23, 1864. Mine Explosion, Petersburg, July 30 (Reserve). Six Mile House, Weldon Railroad, August 18-21. Poplar Springs Church, Peeble's Farm, September 29-October 2. Hatcher's Run October 27-28. Warren's Hicksford Raid December 7-11. Dabney's Mills, Hatcher's Run, February 5-7, 1865. Appomattox Campaign March 28-April 9. White Oak Road March 29. Quaker Road March 30. Boydton Road March 30-31. Five Forks April 1. Amelia C. H. April 5. High Bridge April 6. Appomattox C. H. April 9. Surrender of Lee and his army. March to Washington, D. C., May 2-12. Grand Review May 23. Mustered out—Old members, June 4; Regiment, July 16, 1865.

Regiment lost during service 9 Officers and 138 Enlisted men killed and mortally wounded and 1 Officer and 145 Enlisted men by disease. Total 293.

21st REGIMENT INFANTRY.

Organized at Augusta and mustered in for nine months' service October 14, 1862. Left State for Washington, D. C., October 21. Ordered on reaching Trenton, N. J., to return to New York, and duty at East New York till January, 1863. Embarked for New Orleans, La., January 9. Companies "A," "C," "E," "F," "H" and "K," on Steamer "Onward," reach New Orleans January 31, and moved to Baton Rouge, La., February 3. Balance of Regiment arrive at Baton Rouge February 11. Attached to 1st Brigade, 1st Division, 19th Army Corps, Dept. of the Gulf, to July, 1863.

SERVICE.—Operations against Port Hudson March 7-20, 1863. Duty at Baton Rouge till May. Advance on Port Hudson May 20-24. Action at Plains Store May 21. Siege of Port Hudson May 24-July 8. Assaults on Port Hudson May 27 and June 14. Surrender of Port Hudson July 8. Ordered home July 24. Mustered out August 25, 1863, expiration of term.

Regiment lost during service 1 Officer and 26 Enlisted men killed and mortally wounded and 1 Officer and 144 Enlisted men by disease. Total 172.

22nd REGIMENT INFANTRY.

Organized at Bangor and mustered in for nine months' service October 10, 1862. Left State for Washington, D. C., October 21. Duty at Arlington Heights, Va., till November 3. Moved to Fortress Monroe, Va., November 3, thence to Ship Island, Miss., and New Orleans, La., December 2-15. Attached to Grover's Division, Dept. of the Gulf, to January, 1863. 1st Brigade, 4th Division, 19th Army Corps, Army Gulf, to July, 1863.

SERVICE.—Moved to Baton Rouge, La., January 16, 1863. Duty there till March. Operations against Port Hudson, La., March 7-20. Moved to Donaldsonville March 26, thence to Brashear City. Operations in Western Louisiana April 9-May 14. Teche Campaign April 11-20. Porter's and McWilliams' Plantations at Indian Bend April 13. Irish Bend April 14. Moved to Franklin April 15. Bayou Vermillion April 17. Moved to New Iberia April 25; to Washington May 6, thence to Brashear City May 11-27. Moved to Port Hudson May 28. Siege of Port Hudson June 1-July 8. Assault at Port Hudson June 14. Surrender of Port Hudson July 8. Ordered home July 24. Mustered out August 14, 1863, expiration of term.

Regiment lost during service 1 Officer and 8 Enlisted men killed and mortally wounded and 2 Officers and 169 Enlisted men by disease. Total 180.

23rd REGIMENT INFANTRY.

Organized at Portland and mustered in for nine months' service September 29, 1862. Left State for Washington, D. C., October 18. Attached to Grover's Brigade, Defences of Washington, to February, 1863. Jewett's Brigade, 22nd Corps, to June, 1863. Slough's Brigade, Defences of Alexandria, 22nd Corps, to July, 1863.

SERVICE.—Camp at East Capital Hill till October 25, 1862. Moved to Seneca, Md., October 25, and guard duty along the Potomac River till April 19, 1863. Stationed at Edwards Ferry December, 1862, to April, 1863. Moved to Poolesville April 19, thence to Washington May 5, and to Alexandria May 24. Moved to Poolesville, Md., June 17, thence to Harper's Ferry, W. Va. Mustered out July 15, 1863, expiration of term.

Regiment lost during service 56 Enlisted men by disease.

24th REGIMENT INFANTRY.

Organized at Augusta and mustered in for nine months' service October 16, 1862. Left State for New York City October 29. Duty at East New York till January 12, 1863. Moved to Fortress Monroe, Va., thence to New Orleans, La., January 12-February 14. Attached to 3rd Brigade, 2nd Division, 19th Army Corps, Dept. of the Gulf, to July, 1863.

SERVICE.—Moved to Bonnet Carre, February 26, 1863, and duty there till May. Expedition to Ponchatoula and Amite River March 21-30. Capture of Ponchatoula March 24. Amite River March 28. Expedition to Amite River May 7-21. Civiques Ferry May 10. Advance on Port Hudson May 21-24. Siege of Port Hudson May 24-July 8. Assaults on Port Hudson, May 27 and June 14. Surrender of Port Hudson July 8. Ordered home July 24, and mustered out August 25, 1863, expiration of term.

Regiment lost during service 1 Enlisted man killed and 5 Officers and 185 Enlisted men by disease. Total 191.

A page from Dyer's three-volume *Compendium of the War of the Rebellion*. In it Dyer, a Civil War veteran, compiled a short history of each Union regiment in the war.

As for Civil War pictures in general, the best and most complete set can be found in *The Photographic History of the Civil War*, in ten volumes, edited by Francis T. Miller and published in 1912 by the Review of Reviews Company. This work has been republished in five volumes by Yoseloff.

At the beginning of the war, Matthew B. Brady, the wealthiest and most-noted photographer in America, went off to war. With his great wooden box cameras, glass plates, chemicals, and trained assistants, he followed the Union army from one bloody battlefield to another. Four years and thousands of photographs later, Brady returned to his Washington and New York studios, bankrupt. He never recovered financially from the effects of the war and died in obscurity at seventy-three in Washington, D.C., in 1896. It is Brady's photographs, taken during his four-year stay with the Federal army, that fill the ten volumes of Miller's *Photographic History of the Civil War*. You will probably not find your great-grandfather's picture here. You will find in these ten volumes, however, the finest and most complete set of battlefield photographs, portraits, camp and on-the-march pictures in existence. This is the ultimate source for all Civil War pictorial history. The photographic works of Alexander Gardner, one of Brady's assistants, were printed by Philip and Solomons in 1865 and reprinted by Dover Press in 1959 in a book entitled *Gardner's Photographic Sketch Book of the War*. Most of these pictures are included in Miller's ten volumes. Miller's *Photographic History* has not been reprinted in some time, so you will have to use your library.

The National Historical Society, P.O. Box 8200, Harrisburg, Pennsylvania 17105, has reproduced in six volumes over 4,000 photographic views of the "War between the States," over one-half of which the editors claim have never before been published. This series is entitled *The Image of War: 1861–1865* and is the best and most comprehensive set of photographic books to be printed since the original publication of Miller's ten volumes.

A few days after a bullet from John Wilkes Booth's tiny derringer pistol had smashed into the back of Abraham Lincoln's head, a small body of Union army and navy officers banded together in Philadelphia to act as a guard of honor to the president's body as it lay in state. After the war these men organized the first Civil War veterans' organization, the Military Order of Loyal Legions of the United States (MOLLUS).

"Commanderies" were formed in a number of northern and western states. Sixteen of these commanderies—Indiana, Illinois, Iowa, Kansas, Maine, Massachusetts, Michigan, Minnesota, Missouri, Nebraska, New York, Ohio, Oregon, Pennsylvania, Wisconsin, and the District of Columbia—published numerous books containing rosters, war papers, personal reminiscences, Civil War sketches, and incidents. For those who wish to own their own set, Broadfoot Publishing Company has just reprinted the MOLLUS series in around seventy volumes, including a great three-volume index. Any library can now afford, and should own, a set.

There are several other Civil War publications that may help you in a search for veterans' pictures and stories. *The Confederate Veteran* is without question the most significant nongovernmental publication of its kind concerning the Confederate soldier. It was published monthly in Nashville, Tennessee, from 1893 to 1932, and totals forty volumes. This set of magazines is the largest collection of Confederate memoirs, anecdotes, incidents, and personal stories in existence. Along with the stories are thousands of postwar photographs of veterans and reunion pictures of these old soldiers accompanied by their wives, children, and other relatives. Most of the veterans are identified. For those with Southern ancestors, here is a possibility of locating photographs of relatives about whom you knew only the name. Finally, there are memorial photographs of deceased veterans taken right up to the great depression of the 1930s. At the end of each year's series of magazines there is an index woefully inadequate for modern research. Although *The Confederate Veteran* has been available in microfilm for many years, a reprint of the entire forty-volume series has been completed by Broadfoot Publishing Company of Wilmington, North Carolina. What is especially important is that Broadfoot Publishers has published a splendid, comprehensive, scientific, cross-referenced, three-volume index containing over half a million entries. The old index has less than seventy-five thousand. Until now the greater part of the information lodged in these forty volumes was, for all practical purposes, inaccessible; that is, unless you had the time and patience to thumb through each issue. Now the door has been opened. *The Confederate Veteran* is available from Broadfoot Publishing Company, Morningside Bookshop, and the National Historical Society, among others; the index is available from these booksellers also.

A modern magazine in which you will often turn up photographs not

found in Miller's set is *Civil War Times Illustrated*. The best nonphotographic works are Frank Leslie's *Illustrated History of the Civil War,* now long out of print, and *Harper's Weekly.* Unfortunately, the nonphotographic books will be of limited use to you as a researcher. This is because very few soldiers had their portraits sketched by war correspondents or artists, and most of the battle scenes and camplife drawings of the war contain more artistic fancy than fact.

Personnel Files and Rosters

PERSONNEL FILES, as mentioned earlier, are records that have to do with a soldier's leaves, promotions, illnesses, special assignments, and so on. The personnel records in the National Archives are all based on documents collected by the federal government. Often you will find that these records are not complete. Many times they may give only an enlistment date or the number of a regiment. It is not unusual for the National Archives to have nothing at all on your man. In any case, you should turn to the ever-helpful Dornbusch and to Nevins, Robertson, and Wiley to locate books containing personnel files and rosters. These are the files and rosters that most state archives and other institutions must turn to in order to send you personnel data when you request it from them. You can save time by doing it yourself if a good library is available.

After you have traced six or eight soldiers, you will become aware that your most successful hunts were for Civil War officers. One of the very best publications of officer biographies happened to appear in a paperback edition just after the war. Published by the United States Adjutant General's Office in eight volumes, it was entitled *Official Army Register*

of the Volunteer Force of the United States Army for the Years 1861, 1862, 1863, 1864, 1865. This eight-volume work has been reprinted recently with an additional one-volume modern index by Ron R. Van Sickle Military Books, 22 Montgomery Village Avenue, Gaithersburg, Maryland 20879. These volumes list only the volunteer officers who served in the Union volunteer army, which was comprised of two and a half million men. The contents of the volumes are as follows:

Volume	1	New England
"	2	New York, New Jersey
"	3	Pennsylvania, Delaware, Maryland, District of Columbia
"	4	West Virginia, Virginia, North Carolina, South Carolina, Georgia, Florida, Alabama, Mississippi, Tennessee, Louisiana, Kentucky, Texas, Arkansas
"	5	Ohio, Michigan
"	6	Indiana, Illinois
"	7	Missouri, Wisconsin, Iowa, Minnesota, California, Oregon, Nevada
"	8	The territories of Washington, New Mexico, Nebraska, Colorado, Dakota
		Special Troops: Veterans Reserve Corps, United States Veteran Volunteers, United States Volunteers, United States Colored Troops

This eight-volume set has been reprinted by J. M. Carroll and Company, P.O. Box 1200, Mattituck, New York 11952.

In addition to the above set, the Adjutant General's Office also published seven more volumes entitled *Official Army Register for 1861–1865.* Here you will find biographies of all the regular officers in the Federal army during the war.

Another reference tool is Francis B. Heitman's collection of biographical sketches of all the regular army officers entitled *Historical Register and Dictionary of the United States Army, from Its Organization, September 29, 1789, to March 2, 1903.* The University of Illinois Press has reprinted it, so the book is easily available from most of the book

Cushing, John W. N H. 2 lt 45 inf 21 Apr 1814; 1 lt 1 Sept 1814; resd 7 Jan 1815; [died 3 Mar 1836.]

*Cushing, Samuel Tobey. R I. R I. Cadet M A 1 July 1855 (30); bvt 2 lt 10 inf 1 July 1860; 2 lt 2 inf 19 Jan 1861; 1 lt 14 May 1861; capt 15 Feb 1862; capt c s 9 Feb 1863; maj c s 28 Aug 1888; lt col a c g s 11 Nov 1895; col a c g s 26 Jan 1897; brig gen comsy gen 28 Jan 1898; bvt maj 13 Mar 1865 for fai and mer ser dur the war; retd 21 Apr 1898; died 21 July 1901.

*Cushing, Thomas Humphrey. Mass. Mass. Sergt 6 contl inf Jan to Dec 1776; 2 lt 1 Mass 1 Jan 1777; 1 lt 12 Jan 1778; taken prisoner at —— 14 May 1781; exchanged ——; bvt capt 30 Sept 1783; retained in Jackson's contl regt Nov 1783 and served to 20 June 1784; capt 2 inf 4 Mar 1791; assd to 2 sublegion 4 Sept 1792; maj 1 sublegion 3 Mar 1793; inspr the Army 27 Feb 1797 to 22 May 1798; lt col 2 inf 1 Apr 1802; adjt and I G 26 Mar 1802 to 9 May 1807; col 2 inf 7 Sept 1805; brig gen 2 July 1812; hon dischd 15 June 1815; [died 19 Oct 1822.]

Cushman, Alden G. Mass. 1 lt 4 inf 3 May 1808; dismd 3 July 1809.

Cushman, Allerton Seward. Italy. Mass. Pvt A 6 Mass inf 12 May to 1 Sept 1898; capt c s vols 11 Aug 1898; hon dischd 31 Dec 1898.

Cushman, C. Seth. Me. Wis. 1 lt 14 inf 5 Aug 1861; r adjt 15 Oct 1863 to 6 Dec 1864; resd 6 Dec 1864; [died 9 Jan 1883.]

Cushman, Caleb. Army. Sergt 9 inf 25 June 1812 to Mar 1814; ens 9 inf 30 Mar 1814; 3 lt 1 May 1814; 2 lt 25 July 1814; r adjt Aug 1814 to June 1815; 1 lt 31 Oct 1814; hon dischd 15 June 1815.

Cushman, Charles. Mass. Ens 34 inf 26 July 1814; 3 lt 1 Oct 1814; 2 lt 1 Jan 1815; hon dischd 15 June 1815.

Cushman, Eugene. Pa. Pa. 2 lt 16 inf 17 Dec 1872; 1 lt 15 Mar 1883; resd 1 Oct 1888.

Cushman, Guy. R I. Mo. Pvt and corpl M 1 Mo inf 14 May 1898; tr to D 1 Ohio cav 16 July 1898; hon must out 23 Oct 1898; 2 lt inf 10 Apr 1899; tr to 2 cav 10 May 1899; 1 lt 11 cav 2 Feb 1901.

Cushman, Herbert. Pa. Pa. Cadet naval academy 23 Sept 1862 to 8 Apr 1864; 2 lt 20 inf 23 June 1868; 1 lt 22 Oct 1876; retd 27 Apr 1891.

Cusick, Cornelius Charles. N Y. N Y. 2 lt 132 N Y inf 14 Aug 1862; 1 lt 1 July 1863; hon must out 29 June 1865; 2 lt 13 inf 20 June 1866; tr to 31 inf 21 Sept 1866; tr to 22 inf 15 May 1869; 1 lt 5 Aug 1872; capt 1 Jan 1888; retd 14 Jan 1892.

Custer, Bethel Moore. Pa. Pa. Pvt C 19 Pa inf 18 Apr to 9 Aug 1861; corpl and sergt C 90 Pa inf 17 Sept 1861 to 27 Feb 1864; 2 lt 32 U S c inf 4 Mar 1864; 1 lt 26 Nov 1864; hon must out 22 Aug 1865; 1 lt 11 U S c inf 22 Oct 1865; hon must out 12 Jan 1866; 2 lt 38 inf 28 July 1866; tr to 24 inf 11 Nov 1869; 1 lt 1 Mar 1871; r q m 15 May 1877 to 30 Apr 1880; capt 18 June 1880; bvt 1 lt 2 Mar 1867 for gal and mer ser at James Island S C; died 22 Dec 1887.

*Custer, George Armstrong. Ohio. Ohio. Cadet M A 1 July 1857 (34); 2 lt 2 cav 24 June 1861; 5 cav 3 Aug 1861; 1 lt 17 July 1862; capt a a d c 5 June 1862; hon dischd as a a d c 31 Mar 1863; brig gen vols 29 June 1863; maj gen vols 15 Apr 1865; hon must out of vol ser 1 Feb 1866; capt 5 cav 8 May 1864; lt col 7 cav 28 July 1866; bvt maj 3 July 1863 for gal and mer ser in the battle of Gettysburg Pa; lt col 11 May 1864 for gal and mer ser in the battle of Yellow Tavern Va; col 19 Sept 1864 for gal and mer ser in the battle of Winchester Va; brig gen 13 Mar 1865 for gal and mer ser in the battle of Five Forks Va; maj gen 13 Mar 1865 for gal and mer ser dur the campn ending in the surrender of the insurgent army of northern Va and maj gen vols 19 Oct 1864 for gal and mer ser at the battles of Winchester and Fishers Hill Va; killed 25 June 1876 and his whole command massacred in action with Sioux Inds at Little Big Horn river Mont.

Custer, Thomas Ward. Ohio. Mich. Pvt H 21 Ohio inf 2 Sept 1861 to 10 Oct 1864; 2 lt 6 Mich cav 8 Nov 1864; bvt 1 lt capt and maj vols 13 Mar 1865 for dist and gal con; hon must out 24 Nov 1865; 2 lt 1 inf 23 Feb 1866; 1 lt 7 cav 28 July 1866; r q m 3 Dec 1866 to 10 Mar 1867; capt 2 Dec 1875; bvt capt 2 Mar 1867 for gal and dist con in the engagement with the enemy at Waynesboro Va 2 Mar 1865; maj 2 Mar 1867 for dist con in the engagement with the enemy at Namozine Church Va 3 Apr 1865 and lt col 2 Mar 1867 for dist courage and ser at the battle of Sailors Creek Va; awarded medal of honor 24 Apr 1865 for the capture of a flag at Nanzomine Church Va 2 Apr 1865 and another medal of honor 22 May 1865 for the capture of a flag at Sailors Creek Va 6 Apr 1865; killed 25 June 1876 in action with Sioux Inds at Little Big Horn river Mont.

Custis, George Washington Parke. Md. Va. Cor lht drgs 8 Jan 1799; 2 lt 3 Mar 1799; hon dischd 15 June 1800; [died 10 Oct 1857.]

Custis, Lebbeus. Army. Sergt maj 3 art; 2 lt 3 art 1 Oct 1813; resd 7 Feb 1814.

A page from Francis B. Heitman's *Historical Register and Dictionary of the United States Army.* It lists short biographies of all regular United States Army officers who served from 1789 to 1903. There are other books that list state volunteer officers as well.

companies listed in this book. Not only is Heitman a quick reference, but it could be useful in a very difficult situation. Suppose you have a photograph of a Union officer and on the back is "Captain Sam Jones" and nothing else. Cross your fingers and open up Heitman. If Captain Jones was in the regular army, Heitman will give you a summary of his service. It may be just the lead you will need.

In 1880 Thomas H. S. Hamersly edited and published the *Complete Regular Army Register of the United States: For 100 Years (1779–1879)*. This volume is similar to Heitman's but not nearly so complete. In 1892 and 1893 Lieutenant Colonel William H. Powell of the United States Army published *Officers of the Army and Navy (Regular) Who Served in the Civil War* and a companion volume, *Officers of the Army and Navy (Volunteer) Who Served in the Civil War.* This latter volume is much used by Civil War buffs. Both these books were published by the L. R. Hamersly Company of Philadelphia. For this reason, they are commonly called "Hamersly's" instead of "Powell's" volumes, as they should be.

Similar to Powell's publication is General George W. Cullum's two-volume *Biographical Register of the Officers and Graduates of the United States Military Academy at West Point, New York, from Its Establishment, March 16, 1802, to the Reorganization of 1866-67.* Though no longer in print, it is available in larger libraries.

Lewis Hamersly enters the picture again, not as Powell's publisher, but as the author of his own book, *The Records of Living Officers of the United States Navy and Marine Corps,* Philadelphia, 1870. Here you will find short biographies of United States naval officers from first lieutenant up who survived the battles of the Union navy during the war and were still alive in 1870. John M. Carroll of Mattituck has reprinted this.

For Rebel naval officers the best source is a volume first published by the United States Naval Records Office: *Officers in the Confederate States Navy, 1861-65.* This also has been reprinted by J. M. Carroll and Company, in addition to two other excellent titles that have long been out of print. These are: *A List of Field Officers, Regiments and Battalions in the Confederate States Army, 1861–1865* and *A List of Staff Officers of the Confederate States Army 1861–1865.* Reprints of three Confederate publications concerning the minuscule marine corps are now for sale by Ralph W. Donnelly, 913 Market Street, Washington, North Carolina 27899. They are *The History of the Confederate States Marine Corps, Bio-*

graphical Sketches of the Commissioned Officers of the Confederate States Marine Corps, and *Service Records of Confederate Enlisted Marines*.

If your soldier was a Confederate and you have been told that he was decorated for bravery, that is an easy one to verify. The Confederacy gave only one medal, and that was the Cross of Honor, a reward for exceptional service. Recipients were placed on the Roll of Honor. J. M. Carroll and Company has the book you need to verify that your soldier was selected for this distinction: *The Confederate Roll of Honor: Minutes of the Confederate Congress General Orders Number 64. Richmond, August 10, 1864.* This is the only complete source for names of Confederate soldiers rewarded for bravery.

Chasing your army officer down another avenue, you can try the general state regimental collections. As mentioned earlier, most states have one or a series of books outlining histories of each and every military unit called into state service. Included either in these histories or in separate books are rosters of every soldier and sailor who ever served in any of the state's regiments, naval units, and so forth. These pages and pages of lists of soldiers usually give brief summaries of the service of each man. Many of these rosters will be useful to you if you are at the beginning of your search, for they will give you data on your soldier's regiment, company, enlistment, and termination of service. This information can be readily supplied by the state archives (see Chapter III), but you will have to wait. On the other hand, a quick trip to the library may get you the information in an hour instead of a few weeks. A disadvantage of these rosters is that they, like the regimental histories, are seldom found outside their particular states.

Some of these rosters are huge sets. North Carolina has compiled twelve volumes entitled *North Carolina Troops, 1861–1865: A Roster*. Here are all the names of her servicemen, officers and enlisted men combined. Massachusetts has nine volumes, *Massachusetts Soldiers, Sailors and Marines in the Civil War;* Pennsylvania, five volumes. Michigan has its forty-six-volume *Record of Service of Michigan Volunteers in the Civil War, 1861–1865;* and Louisiana's three volumes are called *Records of Louisiana Confederate Soldiers and Louisiana Confederate Commands*. Appendix B lists the regimental histories and rosters that are, according to the authorities of each state, the most useful.

Once you have obtained all the information you can from the state and

1863. Forwd. from Old Capitol Prison, Washington, D. C., to Fort Delaware, Del., May 7th, 1863. Paroled at Fort Delaware, Del. Exchanged at City Pt., Va., May 23rd, 1863. Rolls from May, 1863, to Feb., 1864, Present. Federal Rolls of Prisoners of War, Captured Spottsylvania C. H., May 12th, 1864. Recd. at Pt. Lookout, Md., from Belle Plains, Va., May 18th, 1864. Forwd. to Elmira, N. Y., Aug. 17th, 1864. Paroled at Elmira, N. Y., Oct. 11th, 1864. Died at Fort Monroe, Va., Nov. 5th, 1864.

Davis, Edward, Pvt. Co. C, 5th La. Infty. En. May 10th, 1861, Camp Moore, La. Apptd. 3rd Corpl. Aug. 18th, 1861; 6th Sergt. Oct. 5th, 1861. Present on all Rolls to Oct., 1862. Rolls Nov. 1862, to April, 1864, Detached on Division Pioneer Corps. Roll April to Aug., 1864, dated Nov., 1864, Present. Born in New York, occupation caulker, single, Res. New Orleans, La.

Davis, Edward, Pvt. Co. A, 1st La. Hvy. Arty. (Regulars). En. May 5th, 1864, Oxford, Miss. Roll for March and April, 1865. Deserted from near Cuba Station April 25th. Appears on Roll, not dated, of Prisoners of War. Surrendered at Post of La Grange, Tenn., May 17th, 1865. Remarks: Left his command at Cuba, Ala., May 1st, 1865. Paroled.

Davis, Elisha W., Pvt. Co. A, 28th (Gray's) La. Infty. En. May 14th, 1862, Monroe, La. Roll for July and Aug., 1863, Detached as Nurse at Hospl., Shreveport, La., from May 15th.

Davis, F. M., Pvt. Co. D, 4th La. Cav. On Roll of Prisoners of War, Paroled at Monroe, La., June 17th, 1865. Res. Union Par., La.

Davis, Fletcher W., Pvt. Co. I, 9th La. Infty. En. Franklinton, La., April 17th, 1862. Record copied from Memorial Hall, New Orleans, La., by the War Dept., Washington, D. C., June, 1903. Born Louisiana, occupation farmer, age when enlisted 16, single, Res. Franklinton, La. Died Charlottesville, Va., May 30th, 1862.

Davis, Florian, Pvt. Co. C, 21st (Patton's) La. Infty. En. Dec. 4th, 1862, Camp Moore, La. Present on Rolls to Feb., 1863. Rolls from Sept., 1863, to Dec., 1863, Absent without leave since Aug. 23rd, 1863. Federal Rolls of Prisoners of War, Captured Vicksburg, Miss., July 4th, 1863. Paroled at Marine Hospl., Vicksburg, Miss., July 17th, 1863.

Davis, Florian, Capt. Co. H, 4th Regt. 1st Brig. 1st Div. La. Militia. On Roll not dated, ordered into service of the State of Louisiana.

Davis, Francois, Pvt. Co. H, 1st La. Hvy. Arty. (Regulars). En. Aug. 6th, 1862, ——, Roll for Nov. and Dec., 1862, Died in Hospl., Dec. 8th, 1862. (Substitute.)

Davis, Francis M., Pvt. Co. E, 12th La. Infty. En. Aug. 18th, 1861, Camp Moore, La. Present to Oct. 31st, 1861. Roll dated June 30th, 1862, Absent. Detailed on guard duty on the railroad above Grenada, Miss., by order Col. Scott, June 16th, 1862.

Davis, Frank A., Pvt. Sergt. Co. F, 3rd La. Infty. En. May 17th, 1861, New Orleans, La. Present on Roll to June 30th, 1861. Roll for July and Aug., 1861, Absent. Nurse at Springfield, Mo. Rolls from Sept., 1861, to April, 1862, Present. Roll for May and June, 1862, Present. Promoted 2nd Corpl., May 16th, 1862. Rolls from July, 1862, to Oct., 1862, Present. Roll for Nov. and Dec., 1862, Resigned as Corpl., Nov. 18th, 1862. Federal Rolls of Prisoners of War. Captured Vicksburg, Miss., July 4th, 1863. Paroled at Vicksburg, July 8th, 1863. Reported in camp for exchange at Natchitoches, La., April 1st, 1864. Rolls of Prisoners of War, Paroled Shreveport, La., June 7th, 1865. Res. Shreveport, La.

Davis, Frank R., Pvt. Co. C, 1st (Nelligan's) La. Infty. En. May 27th, 1861, New Orleans, La. Present on all Rolls to Dec., 1861. Roll Jan. and Feb., 1862, Absent. Guard House. Roll March and April 1862, Present. Rolls June, 1862, to Oct. 31st, 1862, Killed in action June 25th, 1862, near Seven Pines.

Davis, G., Pvt. Cage's La. Cav. Co. F. Federal Rolls of Prisoners of War, Captured East Baton Rouge, La., Jan. 16th, 1865. Transfd. to Vicksburg, Miss., May 11th, 1865, from New Orleans, La.

Davis, G. L., Pvt. Co. D, 25th La. Infty. Roll for March 6th, 1862, to ——, 186—, dated March 26th, —— (only Roll on file). En. March 6th, 1862, Morehouse Par., La. Entitled to bounty of fifty dollars.

Davis, G. L. C., Pvt. Powers Regt. —— Federal Rolls of Prisoners of War, Captured Warrington Co., Miss., Nov. 11th, 1865. Paroled in New Orleans, La., in Military Prison, June 3rd, 1865.

Davis, G. L. C., Pvt. Continental Regt. La. Militia. Roll dated New Orleans, La., Nov. 23rd, 1861, shows him on parade.

Davis, G. L. C., Jr., Pvt. Co. E. Crescent Regt. La. Infty. En. March 5th, 1862, New Orleans, La. Roll for May and June, 1862, Absent. Sick.

Davis, G. M., Pvt. Co. H, 6th La. Cav. On Roll of Prisoners of War, Paroled at Natchitoches, La., June 20th, 1865. Res. Bienville Par., La.

Davis, G. P., Sergt. Co. D. Perkins Battn. Rolls of Prisoners of War, Paroled at Shreveport, La., June 7th, 1865. Res. Denton Co., Tex.

Davis, G. W., Sergt. Co. H, 8th La. Cav. On Roll of Prisoners of War, Paroled Shreveport, La., June 21st, 1865. Res. Bossier Par., La.

Davis, George, Pvt. Doyle's Co. Ogden's La. Cav. On Roll of Prisoners of War, not dated, Captured near East Baton Rouge, La., Jan. 17th, 1865. Transfd. to New Orleans, La., Jan. 31st, 1865.

Davis, George, Pvt. Corpl. Co. G. 5th La. Infty. En. May 29th, 1861, New Orleans, La., age 40 years. Present on all Rolls to Aug., 1862. Sept. and Oct., 1862, Absent. Appointed Oct. 1st, 1862, 2nd Corpl. Sick in Winchester. Nov. and Dec., 1862, Present. Jan. and Feb., 1863, Absent on 30 days' furlough from Feb. 19th, 1863. Roll March and April, 1863, Died at Hospl. in Lynchburg, Va. Born in Ireland, occupation laborer, age when enlisted 32, single, Res. St. Louis, Mo.

Davis, George, 8th La. Infty. Appears on Federal Register of Prisoners, Confined in Guard House, Fort Monroe, Va., June 24th, 1864. Sent to Military Prison, Camp Hamilton, Va., July 1st, 1864. Sent to New York, via Baltimore, July 10th, 1864.

Davis, George, Pvt. Co. I. 15th La. Infty. En. June 9th, 1861, Camp Moore, La. Appears on Report of Deaths, remark: Died Sept., 1861, at Centerville, Va., of typhoid fever. Born in Louisiana, occupation farmer, age when enlisted 26, single, Res. Trinity, La.

Davis, George, Pvt. Co. — Miles Legion La. Militia. On Rolls of Prisoners of War, Captured at East Baton Rouge, La., Jan. 16th, 1865. Sent to New Orleans, La., Jan. 22nd, 1865. Exchanged May 11th, 1865.

Davis, George W., Pvt. Old Co. D. 1st Spec. Battn. (Wheat's) La. Infty. En. June 8th, 1861, Camp Moore, La. On Roll to Aug. 3rd, 1861, Present or absent not stated.

Davis, Ghershom S., Musician Pvt. Cos. K. F. and G. 31st La. Infty. En. Jan. 27th, 1863, Monroe, La. Roll for Jan. and Feb., 1863, Present. Apptd. Chf. Musician, order of Col. C. H. Morrison, Jan. 27th, 1863. Federal Rolls of Prisoners of War show him captured and paroled at Vicksburg, Miss., July 4th, 1863. Paroled at Monroe, La., June 6th, 1865. Res. Ouchita Par., La.

Davis, H. H., Sergt. Co. — Ogden's La. Cav. Federal Rolls of Prisoners of War show

551

national archives and have combed your available libraries for rosters and regimental histories, you will find still more doors to open. There are well over a thousand public and private museums, historical societies, and similar places where millions upon millions of individual items, diaries, letters, and the like, are kept. Some of these may play an important part in your search.

Each state has at least one, and often two, state historical societies that publish journals and have special archives. In addition, there are county, regional, city, and religious historical societies. Then there are special organizations such as the United Daughters of the Confederacy, the Association for the Preservation of Tennessee Antiquities, the Great Plains Historical Association, the Historic Mobile Preservation Society, the Dig and Delve Society (Indiana), and the Association for the Preservation of Virginia Antiquities. The list goes on and on. Most societies have special libraries, many publish documents, and most have special unpublished archives, which could very well be helpful to you in your quest.

Your guide to the historical societies and agencies is the *Directory of Historical Societies and Agencies in the United States and Canada,* published by the American Association for State and Local History, 172 Second Avenue North, Nashville, Tennessee 37201. Most libraries have a copy of this very useful book, but you may buy your own copy by writing to Nashville.

Last, there are countless museums with their historical treasures. There is no telling what might lie in one of these repositories. To give you some idea of the extent of the various holdings, if you were to eliminate the millions of books that are available in these special institutions, there would still remain on their shelves well over one hundred million separate historical items covering over three hundred years of American history.

Without some guide similar to Dornbusch to lead helpless laymen through the libraries, these sources would be useful to very few. In this case the hero who will come to your rescue is the late Philip Hamer, who compiled *A Guide to Archives and Manuscripts in the United States,* Yale University Press, New Haven, 1961. Hamer has listed, state by state and page by page, not only the location of every archive collection, but what it holds by title and subject, giving a brief description of each. His compilation, available in most libraries, is a truly wonderful book and is your

most complete and convenient single-volume guide to all the special collections in the country. Of even greater value in searching for manuscripts is the multi-volumed *National Union Catalog of Manuscript Collections* published by the federal government and kept up to date by it. Because of their cost, these volumes are found only in the larger libraries. If you happen to have any idea of publishing or otherwise publicly presenting your findings on a soldier, sailor, or marine, you really must check Hamer and the *Union Catalog*. These books may tell you if you are about to leave out some useful, and perhaps vital, information. They have even made the difference between the success or failure of professional historians. Think what it could do for you!

Two guidelines similar to Hamer, but not nearly so complete, are the volumes mentioned in Chapter II: Munden and Beers' *Guide to Federal Archives Relating to the Civil War* and Beers' *Guide to the Archives of the Government of the Confederate States of America.* Though these two books are primarily for government archives, they do mention quite a few nongovernment organizations and their holdings. The occasional Civil War searcher will find these books useful, and the professional will find them indispensable.

For those of you who wish to conduct a search on a local level beyond Hamer, there is an endless variety of Civil War related material in town halls, county courthouses, churches, and the like. If you live near the home town of your soldier, a local search is a must. Visit your town or county officials, your local reference librarian, and the nearest historical society leader. If they do not know what is available, then the records must have gone up in smoke in the last courthouse fire or been washed away in some spring flood. Then, too, not all towns or counties cared about their past, so they never bothered to collect or recollect. If you do not know the name of the library near your search area, simply go to the nearest library, which will doubtless have a copy of *The American Library Directory,* where you can get the address of any library in the country.

If, for some reason, you cannot visit the location that you wish, and overworked officials have no time to carry on a correspondence, there are usually professional genealogists and researchers who for a fee will do your research for you. For more information concerning genealogists, you may wish to write to the National Genealogical Society, 4527 17th Street North, Arlington, Virginia 22207.

17 items); Lyle Saxon (La.; author),
1929-45 (3,297 items); Ruth McEnery
Stuart (La.; short-story writer), 1879-
1912 (90 items); Ellsworth Woodward
(La.; artist), 1914-39 (528 items); and
William Woodward (La., Miss.; artist,
prof. of architecture at Tulane Univ.),
1893-1901 (280 items).

Other personal papers include
those of the Favrot family, chiefly
1750-1825 (2,000 items), and of several other distinguished Louisiana
families, 1710-1945. There are also
papers of several Louisiana plantation
owners, mostly for the pre-Civil War
period, and of a few New Orleans mer-
chants. Small groups of papers include
those of a physician, a ship chandler,
an engineer, several lawyers, and numerous other persons.

Also included are a collection of
maps of New Orleans and other parts
of Louisiana, 1608-1938 (749 items);
official records of New Orleans, 1770-
1893 (85 vols. and 1,177 items); records of the Poydraw Home (for or-
phans), 1817-1943 (10,000 items); and
records of a few churches, 1805-1900
(3 vols.). Records relating to science
and art include those of the Louisiana
section of the American Chemical Society, 1906-50 (24 vols. and 580
items); L'Athenée Louisianais, 1876-
86 (215 items); the New Orleans Academy of Sciences, 1858-1949 (252
items); the New Orleans Botanical Society, 1932-41 (1,040 items); and the
Southern States Art League, 1921-47
(907 items). There are also records
of two New Orleans banks, 1827-1903
(166 vols. and 1,114 items); and of the
Street and Electric Railway Union,
1902-40 (39 vols. and 6,961 items).
World War II letters, 1941-45, number 253.

The Louisiana Historical Association Collection, which is on permanent
deposit in the Library's Archives Department, is separately described below under the name of the Association.
See Hist. Records Survey, Guide

for La., pp. 14-16; and De Ricci,
Census, p. 741.

NEW ORLEANS 12

Louisiana Historical Association.
Confederate Memorial Hall, 929
Camp St. Kenneth Trist Urquhart,
Executive Secretary.

Holdings: 150,000 items, 1753-
1920 but primarily 1861-65, relating
chiefly to the Confederate States of
America and the Confederate Army
in the Civil War. Among the records
dated before the Civil War are papers
on the New Orleans campaign, 1814-
15 (554 pieces), including many
morning reports of units of the U.S.
Army and the Tennessee militia; and
papers of Albert Sidney Johnston
(Tex.; U.S. and Confed. Army officer) as U.S. Army paymaster at Austin, Tex., 1848-56 (3,651 pieces). Papers of Jefferson Davis (Miss.; U.S.
Rep. and Sen., Sec. War, Confed.
Pres.), 1845-91 (4,270 pieces), con-
stitute a major group and include
many official documents issued by
Davis as Confederate President.
There are also records of and relating to the executive departments of
the Confederate States, 1861-65 (1,152
pieces); the Confederate Adjutant and
Inspector General's Office (3,702
pieces); the Confederate Navy and Marine Corps (2,725 pieces); several military departments and districts of the
Confederacy (11,356 pieces); Confederate armies and troop units other
than Louisiana units (1,700 pieces);
and Louisiana units in Confederate
service (7,025 pieces). Included also
are manuscripts relating to Civil War
battles (2,000 pieces); maps, plans,
drawings, and plates of uniforms
(500 pieces); miscellaneous account
books, diaries, and reminiscences
from the Civil War period, and papers of Confederate veterans' orga-

Above, and on the following page, are but two of Philip Hamer's thousands of
descriptions of materials held in public and private archives, museums, and
libraries across the country. His book, *A Guide to Archives and Manuscripts in
the United States*, is necessary for a detailed search.

nizations, including the associations of veterans of the Army of Northern Virginia and the Army of Tennessee. (All of the materials described in this entry, while still the property of the Association, are housed in the Archives Department, Howard-Tilton Memorial Library, Tulane University.)

See Hist. Records Survey, Guide for La., p. 4.

—oOo—

Louisiana Historical Society, 521 Carondelet Bldg.

Holdings: Included are transcripts of records in French archives relating to colonial Louisiana, 1678-1769, and to the transfer of Louisiana to the United States, 1803.

See Hist. Records Survey, Guide for La., p. 5; Roscoe R. Hill, American Missions in European Archives (1951), p. 110; and John S. Kendall, "Historical Collections in New Orleans," in N. C. Hist. Review, 7:463-476 (Oct. 1930).

NEW ORLEANS 16

Louisiana State Museum. 709 Chartres St.

Holdings: 400,000 pieces, relating chiefly to colonial Louisiana and to Confederate military history. Included are records of the Superior Council of Louisiana, 1717-69; judicial records of Spanish Louisiana, 1769-1803; some papers dealing with the Battle of New Orleans, 1815; and a large quantity of Confederate military records. Also included are papers of Daniel Clark (La.; Delegate to Cong. from the Terr. of Orleans, merchant); and 5 Civil War dispatch books of Richard Taylor (La.; Confed. Army officer).

See Hist. Records Survey, Guide for La., pp. 6-8; and John S. Kendall,

"Historical Collections in New Orleans," in N. C. Hist. Review, 7:463-476 (Oct. 1930).

NEW ORLEANS 18

Middle American Research Institute Library, Tulane University. Edith B. Ricketson, Institute Librarian.

Holdings: 108 linear ft. and 142 cu. ft., 1348-1960, relating chiefly to Mexico, Central America, and the West Indies. Included are the C. I. Fayssoux Collection of papers of William Walker (La., Calif.; leader of filibustering expeditions to Nicaragua), 1857-80 (551 pieces); a collection of Yucatecan letters, 1778-1863 (856 pieces); treatises on Middle American languages; and extensive government archives, especially for Guatemala.

See Hist. Records Survey, Guide for La., pp. 16-18, its Calendar of the Fayssoux Collection of William Walker Papers (1937. 28 p. Processed), and its Calendar of the Yucatecan Letters (1939. 240 p. Processed); and Marie Hunter Irvine, "Administrative Papers: Copies Relating to New Spain," in the Institute's Miscellaneous Series, No. 5 (1948. 28 p.).

NEW ORLEANS

Newmark Library. 836 Cambronne St.

Holdings: 737 pieces and 1 bundle, 1926-37, consisting of a collection pertaining to the American Old Catholic Church movement in the United States and Canada.

See Hist. Records Survey, Guide for La., p. 11.

Acquiring and Identifying Civil War Equipment

BY NOW, YOU HAVE SEEN how sources such as rosters, personnel files, and official records give the basic facts of a soldier's record. You have also learned how regimental histories, published personal memoirs and biographies, together with pictures and sketches, give life to your soldier and help fill in the blanks left by the official records. There is nothing, however, that will break down the barrier of over one hundred years that separates you from your soldier ancestor faster and more completely than to see and touch the gun that he shot, the clothes that he wore, and the letters that he wrote as he moved from one battlefield and campground to the next. A rifle stock worn smooth and polished bright by constant handling, a diary faded yellow with age whose contents will make a battle as fresh as today, a moth-eaten campaign hat with its cracked and warped leather visor, a sword with a stained blade and battered scabbard—these things will be the ultimate reality between you and your soldier, the final visible remains of your great-grandfather.

Of the millions of families descended from the soldiers in that war, only a bare fraction have such tangible reminders. Fortunately, there is a

This typical Confederate wooden barrel-stave canteen was owned by Private Florian Davis, 21st Louisiana Infantry. Davis was seriously wounded and later captured in the defense of Vicksburg. He was paroled by the federal army on promise never to bear arms against the Union. He kept his promise.

remarkable amount of equipment—guns, saddles, flags, books, knives—left from the war. There is plenty to go around, and the following pages will help relatives and collectors alike in locating and identifying just about any item they may want in the way of equipment similar to that which a particular soldier may have carried.

More than once I have had an enthusiastic relative bring out his grandfather's percussion sporting rifle or Spanish-American War surplus trap-door Springfield and, with misguided pride, parade it in front of me and the assembled guests as the gun that "Granpaw fought the Yankees with." And many more times I have seen and heard how a particular Knights of Columbus sword or a World War I officer's saber led troops that scaled a Union stronghold or sent the Rebels on a reverse trot in some bloody battle. These are not Civil War relics but were manufactured many years later and, as a consequence, they do not have the intrinsic value that a genuine Civil War antique has.

What follows, then, is a brief discussion on how to identify the most commonly used Civil War equipment, uniforms, belts, canteens, and weapons. The procedure will be almost all library or bookshop work to make you your own authority, for there are too many Civil War "experts" whose well-meaning ignorance will lead you into costly mistakes. Then too, unfortunately, the world of antiques has its share of predatory sharks and wolves who possess a razor-keen knowledge of your ancestor's equipment, firmly supported by a lack of moral scruples. These "experts" may strip you of your family treasures for a pittance or sell you a Civil War gun just like your father's father toted into battle, and you may find out too late that it was made up from parts in some basement or that you paid triple the price that you should have. The moral of the story, once again, is that it is far better, lacking honest and knowledgeable friends, to become knowledgeable yourself. It will in all probability save you many a heartache and a few friends, as well.

It would be impossible here to go into a detailed description of the innumerable varieties of Civil War weapons and accoutrements. There are, fortunately, a good many guides that will take you back to the products of the technical world of your ancestors of 1861-65. One of the best present-day general guides to identifying Civil War items is Dr. Francis A. Lord's

Civil War Collector's Encyclopedia. Here is illustrated and described every kind of equipment from great to small: boarding axes, crutches, toothbrushes, pontoons, epaulets, currycombs, hospital cars, coffeepots, tents, and more. This very helpful book is available from the Stackpole Company and is on the shelves of most state libraries.

In 1865 Francis Bannerman established his "Military Goods Business," Francis Bannerman Sons, Inc. His was one of the most unusual business establishments ever organized in the United States. As a result of his shrewd buying not only of Civil War surplus material but of military equipment from all over the world, Bannerman became one of the great private arms suppliers of the world. He purchased an island in the Hudson River four miles north of West Point. He later transported a European castle, stone by stone, across the Atlantic and reassembled it on his island—an island upon and around which he dumped tons of cannon shells as support for his docks and warehouses. Bannerman was accused of being an "outfitter of revolutions," which he vigorously denied. The company has issued illustrated catalogs since 1884, and the most active imagination could not begin to conceive of the thousands upon thousands of varieties of equipment offered over the years. As a company, Bannerman's has declined from its palmy days, and most of the catalogs are costly collectors' items. Bannerman catalogs, which cover weapons from over the entire world, are a prime source for identification of war material of any period of American history from the Spanish conquistadors through the Spanish-American War.

Although "one picture is worth a thousand words" is a hopelessly overworked cliché, it is eminently true when you are trying to describe and identify equipment, particularly guns. James E. Serven's excellent book, *The Collecting of Guns,* is especially good for the beginner because of its many pictures, clear descriptive text, and good advice on what to look for, plus its very useful bibliography. It covers United States firearms from the flintlock to modern weapons. Another classic for beginners and professionals alike is Arcadi Gluckman's *Identifying Old U.S. Muskets, Rifles and Carbines.* Gluckman will help you identify with pictures and text most rifles or muskets from 1803 to the modern army rifle. Gluckman's *United States Martial Pistols and Revolvers* is a splendid companion to

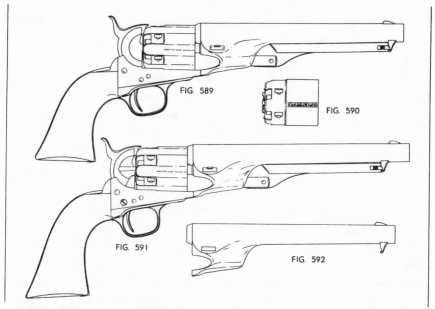

FIG. 589

FIG. 590

FIG. 591

FIG. 592

Model 1860 Armies were a very small number having a round, rebated cylinder of the type which later became standard. This cylinder appears in Figure 590.

Fluted cylinder Army revolvers, in all the variations noted above, dominate the first 2,000 arms of this model produced by Colt. After about serial number 2,000, the fluted cylinder declined substantially in numbers, and by the time 8,000 were turned out, this feature appears to have been completely superseded by the more common round, rebated cylinder. A small number are known in higher serial number ranges, but are believed to have been assembled with surplus parts.

The majority of the first 400 revolvers of this model were manufactured with 7-1/2-inch barrels, with both lengths utilized in nearly equal numbers through the remainder of production of the fluted cylinder types. The short barrel, however, is confined exclusively to these early model revolv-

ers.

The fluted cylinder itself, designed primarily to reduce weight to a minimum, is believed to have been the suggestion of Wade Hampton of South Carolina, a man shortly thereafter to become a renowned Confederate cavalry commander.

In total, a maximum of 4,000 fluted cylinder Army revolvers appear to have been made. A few of these are known handsomely cased in pairs, or with a detachable shoulder stock, and an extreme few have been noted with tinned finishes.

These early Model 1860 Army revolvers, the Type I with "Navy" grips, and Type II comprising the remainder of fluted cylinder models, are believed to have been among the arms delivered under Colt's first contracts for "New Model Holster" revolvers.

• • •

COLT MODEL 1860 PERCUSSION ARMY REVOLVERS, TYPES III and IV

Caliber .44, rifled with 7 grooves having a left-hand twist. Length overall, 14 inches. Weight, 2 pounds, 11 ounces. Single-action.

The 8-inch barrel is round and finished blue. Two marking variations will be found, with the most common being "ADDRESS COL. SAML COLT NEW-YORK U.S. AMERICA". The other stamping is "ADDRESS SAML COLT HARTFORD CT." Both are one-line markings. A brass

blade front sight is 7/16 inch from the muzzle, and the rear sight is formed by a "V" notch in the hammer lip. As on the earlier types, a large loading groove extends completely through the rounded, somewhat streamlined barrel lug as may be seen in Figure 593. A very few of these revolvers, those fitted with detachable shoulder stocks, will be found with a small, two-leaf folding rear sight mortised into the top of the barrel at the breech. This feature is illustrated in

A page from Robert M. Reilly's book, *United States Military Small Arms, 1816–1865*, showing in fine line drawings an accurate, detailed description of the Colt army model 1860 revolver, the most commonly used side arm in the Civil War, North or South. A highly desirable book for identifying rifles and hand guns of the period 1816 to 1865.

Identifying Old U.S. Muskets, Rifles and Carbines and is every bit as competent. Both Serven and Gluckman are now out of print and may be difficult to locate.

James E. Hicks' *Notes on United States Ordnance: U.S. Military Firearms, 1776-1946* is a very useful book embellished by the beautiful and accurate drawings of André Jandot. For the uninitiated, "small arms" refers to long guns and short pistols. An excellent small arms book, and one of major significance, is Robert M. Reilly's *United States Military Small Arms, 1816–1865*. In all the literature in the field I believe there are no illustrations superior to Reilly's, and his text is clear, finely detailed, and authoritative. This is a book that has won deserved praise from the highest circles and is designed for both the rank amateur and the veteran collector. An extensive list of gun and equipment books, both old and new, is found in the back of this work. It is being reprinted by the Gun Room Press, 127 Raritan Avenue, Highland Park, New Jersey 08904. Robert Reilly has just finished a second book of similar quality entitled *American Martial Flintlocks*, a study of flintlock guns and pistols from 1775 to 1850. You may obtain a copy of this book through Mowbray Publishing Company, P.O. Box 460, Lincoln, Rhode Island 02865. Samuel Smith and Edward Bitters' beautiful book on *Historic Pistols: The American Martial Flintlock, 1760–1845* has no equal in its specific field. It is published by the Gun Room Press and distributed by the Rutgers Book Center, 127 Raritan Avenue, Highland Park, New Jersey 08904 (908-545-4344).

There will be times when you are offered a gun with no identification on it other than a maker's name. This is especially true of nonmilitary guns produced earlier in our history. Frank M. Sellers' *American Gunsmiths* (Gun Room Press, also distributed by Rutgers Book Center) is the most complete list of American gunmakers in print today. *The William M. Locke Collection*, edited and published by Robert Berryman (but now out of print), is a photographic representation of what was once perhaps the largest collection of American arms in the country.

Finally, for sheer elegance and beauty there is no equal anywhere in print to R. L. Wilson's *The Colt Heritage: The Official History of Colt Firearms from 1836 to the Present*, published by Simon and Schuster. Here are exquisite color photographs of Colt weapons belonging to Czars

Alexander I and II, Edward VII of England, Horace Greeley, General Custer, and John F. Kennedy, among others.

Should you be lured into buying an antique weapon to identify in addition to your soldier or sailor ancestor, try to buy a complete gun. Missing or broken parts are difficult, if not impossible, to replace. If you have a weapon with missing or broken parts, there is some small hope in Turner Kirkland's catalog, *Dixie Gun Works Incorporated: Black Powder Shooting Supplies and Antique Gun Parts* (Dixie Gun Works, Gunpowder Lane, Union City, Tennessee 38261).

The most authoritative books on Confederate weapons were written in whole or in part by that long-recognized dean of Rebel firearms, William Albaugh III, himself a direct descendant of two Confederate soldiers killed in the war. "Bill" Albaugh and Edward Simmons' *Confederate Arms,* Albaugh's *The Brass Framed Colt and Whitney,* Albaugh and Richard D. Steuart's *The Original Confederate Colt,* and Albaugh, Benet, and Simmons' *Confederate Hand Guns* may have equals, but I have yet to hear of them. Albaugh and his co-writers have done their task so well that subsequent hopeful writers on Southern arms must struggle under the burden of being "better than Albaugh." Broadfoot Publishing Company, through reprints, has now made all of Albaugh's books available.

There are many books and magazines on gun collecting and how to get a duplicate of the gun or pistol used by your ancestor. I will list here only a few of the best. Some are out of print and others are easily available. I shall give an address if the book is still in print and available. The gun collector's bible for identification and evaluation is Norman Flayderman's *Guide to Antique American Firearms and Their Values.* In most cases you can't go wrong with this book. At nearly every gun show that I have attended, most of the dealers and collectors have kept a copy under the table for quick reference. Chapter I discusses "Collecting Firearms." Chapter II, "Values and Condition," will save you many bitter disappointments, and Chapter III offers valuable advice on "Restoration and Fakes." A fine bibliography supports each chapter. With Flayderman available, you won't buy fake or reassembled guns as I have in the past, or pay four times the real value, or sell a family treasure to a fast-talking friend for a fraction of its worth.

The National Rifle Association's two publications, *The American*

Rifleman and *Man At Arms,* also carry lists of addresses of dealers and private collectors from whom weapons and other accoutrements can be purchased, as do a few other publications devoted to weapons. Let me paraphrase a bit of Flayderman. The physical condition of the gun—is it rusted with parts missing, or is it complete with its original parts and free from corrosion? These things are very important. You should understand that the absence of a screw or a difference in sight from one model to the next may mean a difference of hundreds of dollars. As an example, a standard .44-caliber Colt six-shooter issued to your great-uncle may have a smooth round cylinder (the place where you load the shells). The model made just before it looks identical with one exception: it does not have a smooth round cylinder but has a cylinder with a wavy surface made by grooves running down its length. The model with grooves is worth easily three times as much as the smooth-cylinder model. Almost every type of weapon has some distinguishing characteristics that alter its value from model to model, even though the models may look identical to an untrained eye.

The best book on U.S. Army and Militia swords is the old standby, *The American Sword, 1775–1945,* by Harold L. Peterson, the outstanding authority on U.S. "blades." This complete work will identify any U.S. Army sword, as the title suggests, from 1775 to 1945. If you own a sword and do not know how to identify it, most large libraries have a copy of Peterson to which you can refer. Another small but useful book on swords is Ron G. Hickox's *Collector's Guide to Ames U. S. Contract Military Edged Weapons, 1832-1906.* This is good for identification. If yours is a Confederate sword, you will not find your "child" in *The American Sword.* Again, you must turn to William Albaugh; his work on Confederate swords is outstanding. His *Confederate Swords,* together with *Confederate Edged Weapons* and *A Photographic Supplement of Confederate Swords,* is the best you can get for the present.

At present there is no price guide for swords, as there is for guns. Flayderman's sale catalogs will help, as will sales ads in arms magazines such as *Man At Arms* and *The Gun Report.*

Two reliable ways of obtaining a piece of Civil War equipment are through mail-order dealers who specialize in Civil War items, and at local and regional gun shows, where dealers and private collectors display, in

addition to guns, letters, diaries, money, bugles, pictures, and a great variety of other reminders of those far-off days.

By mail order you can purchase almost anything you desire and more than you can imagine. The most important dealers advertise in the leading gun and antique magazines. *The Gun Report,* P.O. Box 111, Aledo, Illinois 61231-0038, is a high-quality monthly magazine dedicated to antique firearms and related items. A similar magazine of equal quality is the well-known *Man At Arms,* P.O. Box 460, Lincoln, Rhode Island 02865. It is a truly fine source of information on antique and modern arms. Both magazines are reliable guides for anyone wishing to purchase Civil War items through the mail. Almost all the nationally known mail-order dealers advertise in them. Although the great majority of smaller dealers are honest and reliable, anyone purchasing by mail an item about which he knows very little might consider using the larger firms first. My only strong caution about mail-order buying by the inexperienced is, do not buy from the private individual selling one or two items from his "own collection" until you have the knowledge and ability to defend yourself. Private buying by mail is a chancy game in which you must carefully decide what risks you are willing to take.

Another satisfactory way of acquiring military equipment is at gun shows, a unique American institution. The better ones are an oriental bazaar and museum all in one. There are at least one or two of these shows somewhere in the United States each and every weekend in the year, and they are growing in popularity.

Local shows are sponsored by local gun clubs or civic organizations and national ones by large gun clubs. Gun shows are almost universally held on weekends, all day Saturday and part of Sunday, closing Sunday afternoon. Most are open to the public for a small fee. The size of a show is determined by the number of tables upon which the articles are displayed. A small local show will have maybe thirty tables. A giant national show will have up to one thousand. The shows are held in well-guarded auditoriums, dining halls, and ballrooms, for at a large show you will see literally several million dollars worth of guns and antiques associated with every aspect of American history. Of course, the emphasis is on the military.

A really good show will have many special educational display tables.

Here you will see Civil War uniforms, Revolutionary War powder flasks, Confederate and Union cannon shells, even Indian artifacts. The variety is endless. The great majority of tables are sales tables operated mostly by small dealers and private collectors, with the larger dealers present in proportion to the size of the show.

Gun shows have the advantage of letting you see any number of swords—or whatever you desire—in a competitive atmosphere, as well as offering you the opportunity to meet some knowledgeable new friends who will be glad to help if they can. Once again, if you have done your homework and know what you are looking for, you might deal at first with small dealers and individuals. But remember, large, well-known dealers with good reputations and a knowledgeable friend to steer you away from fakes or overpriced relics are your best bets.

The Gun Report and *Man At Arms* regularly list all the gun shows occurring throughout the country so that you may see where and when the nearest ones will be held.

While on Civil War magazines, there are a few which stand out, among them *America's Civil War*, published six times a year by The Empire Press, 602 South King Street, Suite 300, Leesburg, Virginia 22075. And how remiss I would be if I did not mention the wonderfully interesting publication called *The North-South Traders Civil War*. It is published every two months and is extremely useful for collectors, historians, and hunters. Here, you can buy, sell, or trade actual battlefield artifacts and read the fascinating stories of how they were found. You can also read articles on arms, equipment, and the war in general. The address is *The North-South Traders Civil War*, Drawer 631, Orange, Virginia 22960.

The American Rifleman, journal of the National Rifle Association, 1600 Rhode Island Avenue, Washington, D.C. 20036, has authoritative articles on antique guns and publishes, as well, supplemental handbooks, reprints, and the like. As an example, for a modest fee you can purchase reprint #7, *Civil War Small Arms,* which gives descriptions and photographs of rifles, carbines, and handguns. Then there is the pamphlet, *Gun Collectors Handbook,* and several others that are useful in the weapons field. *The American Rifleman* also carries advertisements of gun sales and announcements of gun shows.

My first equipment buying experience was a traumatic one. I had longed to own a revolver similar to the one I knew my great-grandfather must have carried in the Civil War. When I saw my first Union army Colt lying in a showcase window, I was literally hypnotized by that vision of delight with its shiny, blued barrel, really beautiful grips, and sleek lines. The gun was at last mine for $200, which I could ill afford. I consulted no books and none of my friends until long after the sale. The gun, I learned later, had been recently reblued; the grips were modern bird's-eye maple, not the old, original Civil War walnut; and the serial numbers did not match, indicating that the gun had been made up from parts both new and old. It took me over a year to sell that bitter monument to my ignorance. I finally sold the gun for $70 and was lucky to do so.

For those of you who are not familiar with the technical aspects of the Civil War, whether it be weapons, tactics, food, or punishment, there are a number of good books on the subject. Mark Boatner's *Civil War Dictionary*, *Historical Times Illustrated Encyclopedia of the Civil War*, edited by Patricia L. Faust and the World Almanac's *The Civil War Almanac* are fine works. Ian Drury and Tony Gibbons's *Civil War Machine* is well written and has the kind of beautifully clear illustrations so often missing in books of this sort. For beginning Civil War buffs, I strongly recommend *Arms and Equipment of the Civil War*, written and illustrated by Jack Coggins. This is probably the best short, fully illustrated look into the Civil War soldier—his life, equipment, and training—in print today. Coggins has the knack of making the difficult and the technical seem obvious and simple, and *everything* is illustrated.

One of the purposes of this chapter has been to steer you around such pitfalls as befell me. You will, if you do much collecting or selling of Civil War equipment, make mistakes, but if you are armed by patient reading and inquiry, all your mistakes will, I hope, be little ones.

Examples
of Research

A NAME IS SELDOM ENOUGH.

My great-grandfather Groene marched away to war in the ranks of an Ohio or Indiana infantry regiment. Or was it an Illinois artillery battery? At any rate, he died during the war and left great-grandmother and two children to shift for themselves. Now, a little over a hundred years later, the family not only can't remember the state from which great-grandfather served, but no one can even recall his first name. Here is a difficult problem. It is a mystery and will probably remain so. I sent letters of inquiry to Indiana, Ohio, Michigan, etc. No great-grandfather. I looked in the *OR* and the *ORN* indexes. Still no luck. Was he an army, navy, or marine officer? I looked in F. B. Heitman's *Historical Register and Dictionary of the United States Army,* H. S. Hamersly's *Regular Army Register of the United States,* and L. R. Hamersly's *The Records of Military Officers of the United States Navy and Marine Corps.* I even looked in *Officers in the Confederate States Navy, 1861–1865,* from the United States Naval Records Office. But great-grandfather never trod the quarterdeck

of a Confederate blockade runner or an ironclad ship. On my search went: libraries, museums, historical societies, special collections. Result— no records of a Groene north, south, or west.

Though my great-grandfather is lost to my family and to history, his is no isolated case. There are literally thousands of soldiers whose records have become misplaced, burned, lost, or otherwise destroyed. These men and their services and sacrifices are, and will probably remain, unknown.

I once owned a Civil War officer's sword with the inscription, "Presented to Lt. J. Wills by Stephen Mercer, Andrew N. Kennedy and others." The blade of this sword might just as well have been inscribed with the rest of the nine hundred or so men of the regiment for all the help it was to me. There were well over three thousand regiments, North and South. I searched through the standard officer biographies mentioned in a previous chapter and then abandoned the hunt. With nothing to go on but a name, you are in an almost impossible situation.

The moral to be drawn by antique collectors from the preceding example is never to consider paying extra for just a name on an antique unless the seller is willing to give you time to try to identify the man. An untraceable name adds nothing to the value of an antique, whether it be weapon, painting, letters, military equipment, or whatever.

Any clue to a name will help.

Occasionally there will be clues that will lead you directly to the identification of a soldier of whom you have only the name. A friend of mine owns a packet of Civil War letters, each signed by William Sullivan, regiment and state unknown. This soldier's frequent mention of friends in a nearby Michigan regiment moved me to write to the Michigan State Archives in Jackson on the chance that Sullivan's regiment was also from Michigan. It proved to be so—the Twenty-sixth Michigan Volunteer Infantry. There then unfolded a poignant story of how a nineteen-year-old farmer, Private William Sullivan, went south to save the Union and died of typhoid fever on the very day that his regiment marched off to battle in Virginia.

A Union officer's sword in front of me has inscribed on the brass throat at the top of the leather scabbard, "Presented to Lieut. C. S. Aldrich by his Ontario Friends." A search of the *OR* and Hamersly for Lieutenant

Aldrich led nowhere, and I was miles from a set of the *Official Army Register of the Volunteer Forces of the United States Army.* The only clue was the word "Ontario." Since the soldier was probably not Canadian, I eliminated Ontario, Canada. That left Ontario, U.S.A., of which there are three or four. I began with Ontario, New York. I drove to the library, strolled over to that well-known six-volume set dedicated to New York Officers and Regiments, Phisterer's *New York in the War of the Rebellion.* (You would have found out about this set of books by referring to Dornbusch's section on New York.) There I found a very brief military biography of Chauncey S. Aldrich. At twenty-seven he enlisted as a first lieutenant of Company B, Eighty-fifth New York Infantry. He later was adjutant of the regiment for a few months, and finally was promoted to captain of Company B. He was mustered out as a major at the end of a three-year enlistment on December 16, 1864. In addition, Phisterer gave a brief history of the battles and casualties of the Eighty-fifth. I could also have found this regiment's history in Dyer's *Compendium.*

The Eighty-fifth up to April 1864, was almost a noncombatant regiment. Then, suddenly, between April 17 and 20 the record lists 543 casualties, all missing! The whole regiment has disappeared at Plymouth, North Carolina. Fascinated by such a drastic change of events, I moved down half an aisle to where the *OR* and the *ORN* were shelved. I reached for the *OR*'s index volume, ran my finger down the pages to Plymouth, North Carolina, and jotted down the volumes in which Plymouth was mentioned. In less than one hour I had uncovered the whole dramatic story.

The Eighty-fifth New York was part of the troops garrisoning the Union fort at Plymouth, North Carolina, on the Roanoke River. On April 17, Confederate troops launched an attack to retake the town and fort, long held by the enemy. On April 19, the great Confederate ironclad battleship *Albemarle*, under Commander Cooke, closed in on the Union ships and fort, sank the U.S.S. *Southfield*, and drove away the smaller defending Union ships. The heavily outnumbered Union troops held to their fort until all hope was lost. Aldrich and his fellow officers handed over their swords to their Confederate captors, and the regiment laid down their weapons. For the Eighty-fifth New York the fighting was over, but

not the dying. The 478 enlisted men were marched to train cars, where they were carried to Georgia and the infamous Andersonville Prison. Here, in less than a year, over half of them died. The twenty-two officers were more fortunate. They were sent south to Charleston and Columbia, South Carolina. All of this history was obtained in one afternoon in the Louisiana State University Library. You could do as much in a smaller library.

My search was not yet ended. I next sent off two NATF forms, one requesting all records, and one requesting any medical records. Two months later in came the results, giving a pension record, any number of muster rolls, a company muster-in-roll, a special muster roll, and last— real pay dirt—a memorandum of prisoner of war records. Captain Aldrich was taken to Columbia, South Carolina, and put in a prison compound. Here he escaped on October 11. One month and three days later he reported for duty in Knoxville, Tennessee.

The last and best part of the story, the escape, still remained to be told. A quick check in Dornbusch showed nothing written by Aldrich, and there were no regimental histories of the Eighty-fifth. I rechecked in Phisterer's *New York in the War of the Rebellion* and copied the officers' roster of the Eighty-fifth to see if any of Aldrich's companions wrote anything. I took the list back to Dornbusch and looked in the New York section. I was in luck. Captain D. A. Langworth of the Eighty-fifth wrote a book entitled *Reminiscences of a Prisoner of War and His Escape*. Maybe Langworth knew Aldrich. Dornbusch indicated that a copy of this book was located in the Library of Congress. DLC was the symbol. Through interlibrary loan I was able to have the book within three weeks. The result: Not only did Langworth know Aldrich; they escaped together! Here was a *whole book* on the perils and narrow escapes of Aldrich, Langworth, and three other officers, which included a photograph of the five taken just after their escape over the mountains of North Carolina into Union-held Tennessee.

Now the sword has a long pedigree and has become an incontestable part of a real-life drama played out over one hundred years ago, beginning with a besieged fort in North Carolina and ending in a Hollywood-scenario escape many months later.

Another weapon I considered buying, also a Union officer's sword,

Prisoner of War memorandum. This states that Capt. C. S. Aldrich of the 85th New York Infantry "escaped at Columbia, S.C., Oct. 11, 1864, and reported [to] Provost Marshal General, Knoxville, Tenn. Nov. 13, 1864." Such information you can get only by a request for "all available information" from the government files. (See page 15.)

Courtesy of the National Archives

"To Lt. C. S. Aldrich from his Ontario Friends" was the only identifying clue inscribed on the scabbard of a Union officer's sword. Research brought out an intriguing story of battle, capture, imprisonment, and finally escape for Captain C. S. Aldrich of the 85th New York Infantry and his companions shown above.

had inscribed on its brass guard "Captain Robert P. Barry"—nothing else. Should I buy it or not? I took a quick look in Heitman to see if by chance it could belong to a regular officer. Luckily, Barry was listed. Now to the Index of the *OR*. There were nine pages of records: Breveted major for gallantry at Murfreesboro, taken prisoner, paroled, commanded the Sixteenth United States Regulars on Sherman's march to and siege of Atlanta. Needless to say, I bought the weapon.

Some years ago I purchased the sword of a George W. Bigham, Captain of Company F, Twenty-sixth Mississippi Infantry. Anxious for information, I dropped a letter to the Mississippi Department of Archives and History and received a quick reply, which stated only that he was Captain of Company F, Twenty-sixth Mississippi Infantry. I opened my copy of Dornbusch and turned to Mississippi. I found that there were no books or articles on the Twenty-sixth. However, at the beginning of each state, Dornbush lists some general references. I copied down the three references for Mississippi and went to my state library. (If you aren't near one, you can get the books by interlibrary loan.) Fortunately, one of the references, *Military Annals of Mississippi,* by John C. Rietti, was on the shelf. Here I struck a gold mine. I learned of Bigham's promotion from second to first lieutenant and of how, after the death of the company captain at the battle of Weldon's Railroad during the siege of Petersburg, he became Captain of Company F. Following this was a detailed history of every battle and skirmish of the Twenty-sixth. On May 5 and 6 Company F and the Twenty-sixth were among General Stone's four Mississippi regiments that finally stood in the Battle of the Wilderness, almost alone in the face of Grant's huge Federal army, until Longstreet came on the field. They fought at Tully's Mill, May 10; Spotsylvania Courthouse, May 22; Hanover Junction, May 23; Cold Harbor, June 2 and 3; Gaines' Mill, May 5; Weldon's Railroad, August 18-19; Fort McRae, October l; and Hatcher's Run, October 27; in addition, they took part in many other skirmishes and fought in the entrenched lines at the final siege of Petersburg. All this I learned the first day at the library. My next step should have been to write for Bigham's pension record, but I had enough to satisfy my curiosity.

In some cases there is almost too much information to bother with.

The National Archives records are very inconsistent in content. The
above items on George W. Bigham, Captain, Co. F, 26th Mississippi illustrate
this point. The "Record" is often found in a soldier's folder.
The list of "Engagements" in which he participated is not often
found so completely done.

Courtesy of the National Archives

The reader will recall the young artillery officer, Ebenezer Mason, in Chapter I, whose battery helped stop the Confederate flotilla as it steamed down the James River on that freezing January night in 1865. At the conclusion of the search for Mason's story I had done the following:

1. Written a letter to the Connecticut State Adjutant General's Office and received one page of records giving his enlistment dates, promotions, discharge, and burial data.
2. Filled out one NATF Form 80 checking pension records and written across the top of the form, "Send all Pension Records." Result: eight pages of pension records giving a complete summary of his service in the First Connecticut Heavy Artillery and a summary of his life as a veteran after the war, including the time, place, and nature of his death.
3. Filled out one NATF Form 80 and written across the top, "Send all military records." Result: thirty-nine sheets of various muster rolls, three sheets of other records.
4. Checked in Dornbusch, which revealed eight references to histories, rosters, etc., of the First Connecticut Heavy Artillery. Made a trip to my library, where an interlibrary loan request was mailed to the Connecticut State Library for John C. Taylor's *History of the First Connecticut Artillery and of the Siege Trains of the Armies Operating Against Richmond, 1862–1865*. On receiving the book, I copied eight pages of notes relating directly to Mason. Left untouched were the seven other books, etc., on the First Artillery.
5. Checked the *OR* and *ORN*, which revealed eighteen pages of reports and records relating to Mason and his participation in various engagements.
6. Checked Dyer's *Compendium*, which gave one paragraph of the history of the regiment. In total I collected seventy-eight pages of records. There are undoubtedly many more pages on Mason in the seven Dornbusch references that I did not bother to send for, but seventy-eight pages of references to my soldier and his sword are quite enough for me for now. I'll tackle the rest on some distant rainy day.

There are times in historical research when nothing seems to help, even when the complete name and regiment are known. I know of a battered

and bloody battle drum with "Chester Chitfield, 29 Ohio Voluntary Infantry," plainly written on the inside of the rounded body. Written on the snarehead side of the drum are the proud but faded words: "Fredericksburgh Va. Dec. 13-14, 1862," and "Chancellorsville, May 3rd 1863." One-third of the drum or batterhead side is stained with blood. There is no record of a Chester Chitfield on the existing rolls of the Twenty-ninth Ohio Volunteer Infantry, yet the drum is authentic beyond the shadow of a doubt.

For over two decades and through three editions of this book I honestly believed the above paragraph about "Chester Chitfield" to be accurate. Not long ago a graduate student, who is also a friend, proceeded to unravel the mystery of the bloody drum. With the help of a little volume by E. Kay Kirkham entitled *The Handwriting of American Records for a Period of 300 Years* (Everton Publishers, P.O. Box 368, Logan, Utah 84321), he was able to decipher the writing more accurately. He read "Eugene A. Chatfield 27th C.V.I." I rushed the new name and unit off to Hartford, Connecticut. In about two weeks back came the answer, "Eugene A. Chatfield, Musician, Company I, Twenty-seventh Connecticut Infantry." The Twenty-seventh Volunteer Infantry was one of those short, nine-month outfits, but they got to "see the elephant," for they marched straight into the hell of Fredericksburg, Chancellorsville, and Gettysburg before being discharged shortly after that battle. How could I have misread "Chester" for "Eugene"? Old script *J*'s, *I*'s, *E*'s, and *S*'s are very difficult to distinguish. Then there are the recorders to consider—their education, health, nativity, and intelligence all contribute to a nonuniform recording and script style. Well, there is always Kirkham to help you out. Then there are the times when the records absolutely contradict one another, as the following example illustrates.

The grandfather of an acquaintance of mine was in the Rebel army that defended Vicksburg against Grant's besieging army in 1863. His name does not appear on the rolls of the Confederate regiment in which the family knows that he served. This lack of records means nothing since the grandfather's name and regiment are chiseled in stone on one of Vicksburg's main monuments for all the world to see. The simple fact, as I have said before, is that records do get lost by the tens of thousands. If

you cannot find information on your soldier, it does not mean that he never existed. It means only that he was, historically speaking, shot dead in the records office. So you must brace yourself for occasional failures and dead ends.

Often a family's handed-down history will appear to have hardly a word of truth in it. A beautiful Colt Civil War army revolver I own came with a wonderful story. The owner, Captain Charles P. Crandall, had been on the personal staff of Robert E. Lee. Crandall, I was told, was a trusted friend whom the great general sent upon many an important mission, both as his courier and as his personal representative. This story was related by Crandall's aging widow in the depression days of the 1930s. She was selling the last mementos of her long-dead husband to hold her poor old body and soul together. A search into the records found that Charles P. Crandall was a private in the First Virginia Artillery—that and nothing more.

A year or so ago an old friend of mine, Paul Hobday, died at the age of ninety-three. Paul's father, Charles Hobday, had been a trooper in the Fifth Virginia Cavalry. On many a wintry day I would sit by Paul's chair in front of an old oil stove and listen to him retell the tales of that far-off war recounted to him by his father. I would occasionally glance over my shoulder to catch a glimpse of an old cavalry sword that was hanging over the door behind us. Perhaps it was to reassure myself that what I was hearing was really true. Maybe it was simply to lay my eyes upon that old weapon to make more real the story being told me by an old man who I knew would soon be dead. At any rate, I occasionally broke the spell to jot a few quick notes. Later I collected a bit more family data. Paul died, and I bought that sword above the door. All the records that I could ever obtain of Paul's father were two pages of a company muster roll stating that Private Charles E. Hobday transferred from the Sixty-first Virginia Militia to the Fifth Virginia Cavalry on May 14, 1862. How many of the stories that Paul told me as we sat together in front of that stove while the cold January winds swept up the East River from Mobjack Bay, Virginia, were true, I shall never know. I shall never know since the records are silent and I must trust to an old man's memory that most likely quickened and brightened each story with its retelling. I shall never forget those days, as you will never forget stories told to you by your

grand old folk, and you, like me, may be reluctant to dig into the cold facts, for so often dreams are a better reality. But you must, you know, for grandfather may not have told half the story, and that untold half may be the best part of all.

This picture shows the strokes of the sticks in the center of the drum and the bloodstains of the drummer around the edge. On the other side of the drum is written, "Fredericksburgh Va. Dec. 13–14, 1862," and "Chancellorsville, May 3rd 1863." Inside the drum in pencil is inscribed the name "Eugene A Chatfield, 27th C.V.I." Chatfield was the drummer for Company I, Twenty-seventh Connecticut Volunteer Infantry. The Twenty-seventh fought at Fredericksburg, Chancellorsville, and Gettysburg. He survived the war.

Institutions That Hold Microfilmed Service Records from the National Archives

ALABAMA
  Confederate Volunteers
    Birmingham Public Library, Birmingham
    United Daughters of the Confederacy, Richmond, Virginia
  Union Volunteers*
    Auburn University, Auburn
    Birmingham Public Library, Birmingham

ARIZONA TERRITORY
  Confederate Volunteers
    Arizona State College, Flagstaff
    Arizona Historical Foundation, Tempe
    Arlington State College, Tennessee
    Fort Lewis College, Durango, Colorado
    Salt Lake City Genealogical Society, Salt Lake City, Utah
    United Daughters of the Confederacy, Richmond, Virginia
    University of Arizona, Tucson

*Union Volunteers refers to men from Southern states who fought in the ranks of the Union army.

ARKANSAS
    Confederate Volunteers
        Arkansas History Commission, Little Rock
        United Daughters of the Confederacy, Richmond, Virginia
    Union Volunteers
        Arkansas History Commission, Little Rock

FLORIDA
    Confederate Volunteers
        Hillsborough County Historical Commission, Tampa
        United Daughters of the Confederacy, Richmond, Virginia
        University of Florida, Gainesville
    Union Volunteers
        University of Florida, Gainesville

GEORGIA
    Confederate Volunteers
        Department of Archives and History, Atlanta
        United Daughters of the Confederacy, Richmond, Virginia
    Union Veterans
        Department of Archives and History, Atlanta

KENTUCKY
    Confederate Volunteers
        Murray State University, Murray
        United Daughters of the Confederacy, Richmond, Virginia

LOUISIANA
    Confederate Volunteers
        Division of Archives, Records Management, and History,
            Baton Rouge
        Louisiana Civil War Centennial Commission, Baton Rouge
        Louisiana State University, Baton Rouge
        New Orleans Public Library, New Orleans
        United Daughters of the Confederacy, Richmond, Virginia

Union Volunteers
    Division of Archives, Records Management, and History,
      Baton Rouge
    Louisiana State University, Baton Rouge
    New Orleans Public Library, New Orleans

MARYLAND
  Confederate Volunteers
    Maryland Historical Society, Baltimore
    United Daughters of the Confederacy, Richmond, Virginia

MISSISSIPPI
  Confederate Volunteers
    Department of Archives and History, Jackson
    Louisiana State University, Baton Rouge, Louisiana
    United Daughters of the Confederacy, Richmond, Virginia
    University of Southern Mississippi, Hattiesburg
  Union Volunteers
    California State College, Hayward, California
    Louisiana State University, Baton Rouge, Louisiana
    University of Southern Mississippi, Hattiesburg

MISSOURI
  Confederate Volunteers
    St. Louis Public Library, St. Louis
    United Daughters of the Confederacy, Richmond, Virginia
  Union Volunteers
    St. Louis Public Library, St. Louis

NEW MEXICO TERRITORY
  Union Volunteers
    Genealogical Society of the Church of Jesus Christ of Latter Day
      Saints, Salt Lake City, Utah
    University of New Mexico, Albuquerque

NORTH CAROLINA
Confederate Volunteers
Division of Archives and History, Department of Cultural
Resources, Raleigh
United Daughters of the Confederacy, Richmond, Virginia
Union Volunteers
Division of Archives and History, Department of Cultural
Resources, Raleigh

SOUTH CAROLINA
Confederate Volunteers
United Daughters of the Confederacy, Richmond, Virginia

TENNESSEE
Confederate Volunteers
Cossitt-Goodwyn Libraries, Memphis
Tennessee State Library and Archives, Nashville
United Daughters of the Confederacy, Richmond, Virginia
Union Volunteers
Tennessee State Library and Archives, Nashville

TEXAS
Confederate Volunteers
United Daughters of the Confederacy, Richmond, Virginia
Union Volunteers
Rice University, Houston

UTAH
Union Volunteers
Ricks College, Rexburg, Idaho
Salt Lake City Genealogical Society, Salt Lake City
University of Nevada, Reno, Nevada

VIRGINIA
Confederate Volunteers
United Daughters of the Confederacy, Richmond
Virginia Polytechnic Institute, Blacksburg
West Virginia Department of Culture and History,
Charleston, West Virginia
Union Volunteers
West Virginia Department of Culture and History, Charleston,
West Virginia
Confederate General and Staff Officers and Nonregimental Enlisted Men
Georgia Department of Archives and History, Atlanta, Georgia
United Daughters of the Confederacy, Richmond, Virginia
University of British Columbia, Vancouver, B.C.
South Carolina Department of Archives and History, Columbia,
South Carolina
Organizations Raised Directly by the Confederate Government
Georgia Department of Archives and History, Atlanta, Georgia
United Daughters of the Confederacy, Richmond

Appendix B
Source Books For Regimental Histories and Rosters*

ALABAMA

Brewer, Willis. *Alabama, Her History, Resources, War Record, and Public Men, from 1540 to 1872.* Montgomery, Alabama: Barrett and Brown, 1872.

ARIZONA

See adjacent states.

ARKANSAS

Arkansas Adjutant General's Office. *Report of the Adjutant General of the State of Arkansas, for the Period of the Late Rebellion, and to November 1, 1866.* Washington, D.C.: Government Printing Office, 1867.

Ferguson, John L., ed. *Arkansas and the Civil War.* Little Rock, Arkansas: Pioneer Press, 1965.

Wright, Marcus J. *Arkansas in the War 1861–1865.* Batesville, Arkansas: Independence County Historical Society, 1963.

---

*This list is a quick guide for those who wish the most complete and authoritative state regimental and state roster source books in one or several volumes. They have been recommended chiefly by the various state archives and historical societies. For detailed works see C. E. Dornbusch, *Military Bibliography of the Civil War,* and Nevins, Robertson, and Wiley, *Civil War Books.*

Many of these references are not definitive due to inconsistencies plus the continual outpouring of new research materials. No single book gives the complete answer nor probably ever will. Check with the state archivist or state librarian if a reference yields little help.

CALIFORNIA

Adjutant General's Office. *Official Army Register of the Volunteer Force of the United States Army for the Years 1861, '62, '63, '64, '65.* Part VII. Washington, D.C.: Government Printing Office, 1869.

Hunt, Aurora. *The Army of the Pacific.* Glendale, California: A. H. Clarke Co., 1951.

Orton, Richard H., compiler. *Records of California Men in the War of the Rebellion, 1861–1867.* Sacramento, California: State Printer, 1890.

Parker, J. Carlyle, compiler. *A Personal Name Index to Orton's "Records of California Men in the War of the Rebellion, 1861–1867."* Gale Genealogy and Local History Series, Vol. 5. Detroit: Gale Research Company, 1978.

COLORADO

Adjutant General's Office. *Official Army Register of the Volunteer Force of the United States Army for the Years 1861, '62, '63, '64, '65.* Part VIII. Washington, D.C.: Government Printing Office, 1869.

Colorado State Archives and Public Records. Department of Military Affairs. *Biennial Reports of the Adjutant General, 1861–1865.* Denver, Colorado: Adjutant General's Office, 1866.

Hollister, Ovando. *Colorado Volunteers in New Mexico, 1862.* Chicago, Illinois: R. R. Donnelley, 1962.

Nankivell, John H. *History of the Military Organizations of Colorado, 1860–1935.* Denver, Colorado: W. H. Kistler Stationery Co., 1935.

CONNECTICUT

Adjutant General's Office. *The Record of Connecticut Men in the War of Rebellion, 1861-1865.* Hartford, Connecticut: Press of Case, Lockwood and Brainard Co., 1889.

DELAWARE
Adjutant General's Office. *Official Army Register of the Volunteer Forces of the United States Army for the Years 1861, '62, '63, '64, '65.* Part III. Washington, D.C.: United States Government Printing Office, 1869.

Scharf, J. Thomas. *History of Delaware, 1609–1888.* Two volumes. Philadelphia, Pennsylvania: L. J. Richards and Co., 1888.

FLORIDA
Robertson, Frederick L. *Soldiers of Florida in the Seminole Indian, Civil and Spanish-American Wars.* Live Oak, Florida: Democrat Book and Job Print., 1909.

GEORGIA
Dornbusch, C. E. *Military Bibliography of the Civil War.* Volume 2, Georgia. New York: New York Public Library, 1967.

Garman, Edward. "Materials for the Writing of Histories of Georgia Confederate Regiments: A Bibliographic Study." Master's thesis, University of Georgia, n.d.

Henderson, Lillian. *Roster of the Confederate Soldiers of Georgia.* Six volumes. Hapeville, Georgia: Longino and Porter, 1959-64.

ILLINOIS
Reece, J. N. *Adjutant General's Reports for the Years 1861-66.* Eight volumes. Springfield, Illinois: Phillips Bros., State Printers, 1900-02.

INDIANA
McCormick, David. *Indiana Battle Flags.* Indianapolis, Indiana: Indiana Battle Flag Commission, 1929.

Terrell, W. H. H. *Adjutant General's Report.* Eight volumes. Indianapolis, Indiana: Alexander H. Conner, State Printer, 1865-69.

Turner, Ann. *Guide to Indiana Civil War Manuscripts.* Indianapolis, Indiana: Indiana Civil War Centennial Commission, 1965.

IOWA
Petersen, William J. *Iowa History Reference Guide.* Iowa City, Iowa: The State Historical Society of Iowa, 1952.

Thrift, William H. *Roster and Record of Iowa Soldiers in the War of the Rebellion.* Six volumes. Des Moines, Iowa: E. H. English, State Printer, 1908.

KANSAS
Adjutant General. *Report of the Adjutant General of the State of Kansas, 1861-65.* Topeka, Kansas: Kansas State Print. Co., 1896.

KENTUCKY
Adjutant General's Office. *Report of the Adjutant General of the State of Kentucky. Confederate Kentucky Volunteers, War 1861–1865.* Two volumes. Frankfort, Kentucky: State Journal Co., Printers, 1915-18.

_____. *Report of the Adjutant General of the State of Kentucky. Union Kentucky Volunteers, 1861–1865.* N.p., n.d.

Speed, Thomas, et al. *The Union Regiments of Kentucky.* Louisville, Kentucky: Union Soldiers and Sailors Monument Association, Courier-Journal Job Print. Co., 1897.

LOUISIANA
Bartlett, Napier. *Military Record of Louisiana.* New Orleans, Louisiana: L. Graham and Co., Printers, 1875.

Bergeron, Arthur W., Jr. *Guide to Louisiana Confederate Military Units, 1861–1865.* Baton Rouge, Louisiana: Louisiana State University Press, 1989.

Booth, Andrew. *Records of Louisiana Confederate Soldiers and Louisiana Confederate Commands.* New Orleans, Louisiana: Military Record Commission, 1920.

MAINE

Adjutant General's Office. *Annual Report 1861-66.* Seven volumes. Augusta, Maine: Stevens and Sayward, 1862-67.

Jordan, W. B. *Maine in the Civil War. A Bibliographic Guide.* Portland, Maine: Maine Historical Society, n.d. (from Maine Historical Society, 485 Congress Street, Portland, Maine.)

Whitman, E. S., and Charles H. True. *Maine in the War for the Union. History of the Part Borne by Maine Troops in the Suppression of the American Rebellion.* Lewiston, Maine: Nelson Dingley, Jr., and Co., Publishers, 1865.

MARYLAND

Goldsborough, William W. *The Maryland Line in the Confederate Army, 1861–1865.* Baltimore, Maryland: Press of Guggenheimer, Weil and Co., 1900.

State Commissioners. *The History and Roster of Maryland Volunteers, War of 1861-5.* Volumes 1 and 2. Baltimore, Maryland: Press of Guggenheimer, Weil and Co., 1898-99.

MASSACHUSETTS

Adjutant General's Office. *The Massachusetts Soldiers, Sailors and Marines in the Civil War.* Eight volumes. Norwood, Massachusetts: At the Norwood Press, 1931.

Higginson, Thomas W. *Massachusetts in the Army and Navy During the War of 1861-1865.* Two volumes. Boston, Massachusetts: Wright & Potter, 1895-96.

MICHIGAN

Brown, George H., ed. *Record of Service of Michigan Volunteers in the Civil War, 1861-1865.* 46 volumes. Kalamazoo, Michigan: Ihling Bros. and Everard Printers, 1905.

Lanman, Charles. *The Red Book of Michigan: A Civil, Military and Biographical History*. Detroit, Michigan: E. B. Smith and Co., 1871.

Robertson, John. *Michigan in the War*. Lansing, Michigan: W. S. George and Co., State Printers, 1882.

MINNESOTA
Board of Commissioners. *Minnesota in the Civil War and Indian War, 1861–1865*. Two volumes. St. Paul, Minnesota: Pioneer Press Co., 1890-93.

MISSISSIPPI
Rietti, John C. *Military Annals of Mississippi*. Jackson, Mississippi: Published by the author, 1895.

Rowland, Dunbar. *Military History of Mississippi, 1803–1898*. Spartanburg, South Carolina: Reprint Company, 1978.

MISSOURI
Adjutant General of Missouri Reports 1863–1865.

Dyer, Frederick H. *A Compendium of the War of the Rebellion*. Volume III. New York: Thomas Yoseloff, 1959.

United States Records and Pension Office. *Organization and Status of Missouri Troops (Union and Confederate) in Service During the Civil War*. Washington, D.C.: Government Printing Office, 1902.

NEVADA
Adjutant General's Office. *Official Army Register of the Volunteer Force of the United States Army for the Years 1861, '62, '63, '64, '65*. Part VII. Washington, D.C.: Government Printing Office, 1867.

_____. *Report of The Adjutant General of the State of Nevada for 1865, Journal of the Senate During the Second Session of the Legislature of the State of Nevada, 1866*. Carson City, Nevada: John Church, State Printer, 1866.

Dornbusch, C. E. *Military Bibliography of the Civil War.* Volume II, Nevada. New York: The New York Public Library, 1967.

NEW HAMPSHIRE
Ayling, Augustus. *Revised Register of New Hampshire Soldiers and Sailors in the War of the Rebellion.* Concord, New Hampshire: Ira C. Evans, Public Printer, 1895.

NEW JERSEY
Foster, John Y. *New Jersey and the Rebellion: A History of the Service of the Troops and People of New Jersey in Aid of the Union Cause.* Newark, New Jersey: Martin R. Dennis and Co., 1868.

Sinclair, Donald A. *The Civil War and New Jersey.* New Brunswick, New Jersey: Published by the Friends of the Rutgers University Library for the New Jersey Civil War Centennial Commission, 1968.

Stryker, William. *Records of Officers and Men of New Jersey in the Civil War, 1861–1865.* Trenton, New Jersey: J. L. Murphy, 1876.

NEW MEXICO
Dornbusch, C. E. *Military Bibliography of the Civil War.* Volume II, New Mexico. New York: The New York Public Library, 1967.

Adjutant General's Office. *Official Army Register of the Volunteer Force of the United States Army for the Years 1861, '62, '63, '64, '65.* Part VIII. Washington, D.C.: Government Printing Office, 1869.

NEW YORK
Dornbusch, C. E. *Military Bibliography of the Civil War.* Volume I, New York. New York: The New York Public Library, 1967.

Phisterer, Frederick. *New York in the War of the Rebellion, 1861–1865.* Six volumes. Albany: J. B. Lyon Co., State Printers, 1912.

NORTH CAROLINA

Biographical Sketches of the Commissioned Officers of the Confederate States Marine Corps. (Reprint) 2d ed. Washington, North Carolina: Ralph W. Donnelly, 1983.

Bradley, Stephen E., ed. *North Carolina Confederate Militia Officers Roster: As Contained in the Adjutant-General's Officers Roster.* Wilmington, North Carolina: Broadfoot Publishing Company.

Clark, Walter, editor. *Histories of the Several Regiments and Battalions in the Great War, 1861–1865.* Raleigh and Goldsboro: State of North Carolina, 1901.

The History of the Confederate States Marine Corps. (Reprint) Washington, North Carolina: Ralph W. Donnelly, 1976.

Jordan, Weymouth T., and Louis H. Manarin. *North Carolina Troops 1861–1865.* Thirteen volumes. Raleigh, North Carolina: North Carolina Division of Archives and History, in publication.

Moore, John W. *Roster of North Carolina Troops in the War Between the States.* Raleigh, North Carolina: Ashe and Gatling, 1882.

Service Records of Confederate Enlisted Marines. (Reprint) Washington, North Carolina: Ralph W. Donnelly, 1979.

NORTH DAKOTA
See South Dakota.

OHIO
Official Roster of Soldiers of the State of Ohio in the War of the Rebellion. Twelve volumes. Akron, Ohio: Werner Company, 1886-95.

Reid, Whitelaw. *Ohio in the War.* Two volumes. Cincinnati, Ohio: Moore, Wilstach and Baldwin, 1868.

OKLAHOMA

See adjacent states and territories in Dornbusch and Nevins, Robertson, and Wiley.

Foreman, Grant. *History of the Service and List of Individuals of the Five Civilized Tribes in the Confederate Army.* Two volumes. Oklahoma City, Oklahoma: Oklahoma Historical Society, 1928.

Microfilmed record of "Application of Indigent Soldier or Sailor of the Confederacy for Pension under the Act of February 25th, 1915."

PENNSYLVANIA

Bates, Samuel P. *History of Pennsylvania Volunteers, 1869-1871.* Reprint, fourteen volumes including a new four-volume index. Wilmington, North Carolina: Broadfoot Publishing Company.

RHODE ISLAND

Barker, Harold R. *History of the Rhode Island Combat Units in the Civil War, 1861-1865.* Providence, Rhode Island: H. R. Barker, 1964.

Dyer, Elisha. *Adjutant General's Report of 1865.* Providence, Rhode Island: C. L. Freeman and Sons, 1893-95.

SOUTH CAROLINA

Cote, Richard N. *Local and Family History in South Carolina: A Bibliography.* Easley, South Carolina: Southern Historical Press, 1981.

Dornbusch, C. E. *Military Bibliography of the Civil War.* Volume II, South Carolina. New York: The New York Public Library, 1967.

Easterby, J. H., and Noel Polk. *Guide to the Study and Reading of South Carolina History.* Spartanburg, South Carolina: Reprint Company, 1975. (For regimentals.)

National Archives and Records Service Microcopy 267, *Compiled Service Records of Confederate Soldiers Who Served in Organizations from the State*

of South Carolina, National Archives. (For rosters of South Carolina soldiers.)

SOUTH DAKOTA

English, M. A. "Dakota's First Soldiers: History of the First Dakota Cavalry, 1862-1865," *South Dakota Historical Collections.* Volume IX. (1918) pp. 241-335.

Jones, Robert Huhn. *The Civil War in the Northwest: Nebraska, Wisconsin, Iowa, Minnesota and the Dakotas.* Norman, Oklahoma: University of Oklahoma Press, 1960.

Monaghan, Jay. *The Civil War on the Western Border.* Boston, Massachusetts: Little, Brown and Co., 1955.

TENNESSEE

Adjutant General's Office. *Report of the Adjutant General of the State of Tennessee, of the Military Forces of the State from 1861 to 1866.* Nashville, Tennessee: Mercer, State Printer, 1866. (Union forces.)

Lindsley, John B. *The Military Annals of Tennessee.* Nashville, Tennessee: J. M. Lindsley and Company, 1886.

Tennesseans in the Civil War. Nashville, Tennessee: Civil War Centennial Commission, 1964.

Tennesseans in the Civil War, Part I and *Part II.* Nashville, Tennessee: Civil War Centennial Commission, 1965.

TEXAS

Dornbusch, C. E. *Military Bibliography of the Civil War.* Volume II, Texas. New York: The New York Public Library, 1967.

Fitzhugh, Lester N., compiler. *Texas Batteries, Battalions, Regiments, Commanders, and Field Officers, Confederate States Army, 1861-1865.* Midlothian, Texas: Mirror Press, 1959.

Report of the Adjutant General of the State of Texas, 1873.

Wright, Marcus J. (Simpson, Harold B., ed.). *Texas in the War, 1861–1865.* Hillsboro, Texas: Hill Jr. College Press, 1965.

UTAH

Dornbusch, C. E. *Military Bibliography of the Civil War.* (See adjacent western states and territories). Volumes I and II. New York: The New York Public Library, 1967.

VERMONT

Adjutant General. *Revised Roster of Vermont Volunteers of the Civil War.* Montpelier, Vermont: Press of the Watchman Publishing Co., 1892.

VIRGINIA

✔ Dornbusch, C. E. *Military Bibliography of the Civil War.* Volume II, Virginia. New York: The New York Public Library, 1967.

✔ Howard, H. E., ed. *Virginia Regimental Histories Series.* Projected 135 volumes. Lynchburg, Virginia: H. E. Howard, Inc., 1993–97.

✔ Wallace, Lee A. *A Guide to Virginia Military Organizations, 1861-65.* Lynchburg, Virginia: H. E. Howard, Inc., 1985.

WEST VIRGINIA

Adjutant General's Office. *Annual Report of the Adjutant General of the State of West Virginia, for the Year Ending December 31, 1864.* Wheeling, West Virginia: John F. M'Dermot, Public Printer, 1865.

_____. *Annual Report of the Adjutant General of the State of West Virginia, for the Year Ending December 31, 1865.* Wheeling, West Virginia: John Frew, Public Printer, 1866.

Lang, Theodore K. *Loyal West Virginia from 1861 to 1865.* Baltimore, Maryland: Deutsch Publishing Co., 1895.

Shetler, Charles. *West Virginia Civil War Literature.* Morgantown, West Virginia. West Virginia University Library, 1963.

WISCONSIN

Adjutant General's Office. *Roster of Wisconsin Volunteers, War of the Rebellion, 1861–1865.* Madison, Wisconsin: Democratic Printing Co., 1886. Two volumes. Index, *Wisconsin Volunteers, War of the Rebellion, 1861-1865.* Madison, Wisconsin: Democratic Printing Co., 1914.

Love, William D. *Wisconsin in the War of the Rebellion.* Chicago, Illinois: Church and Goodman, 1866.

Quiner, Edwin B. *Military History of Wisconsin.* Chicago, Illinois: Clarke and Co., 1866.

Appendix C
Source Books for
Identifying Civil War
Weapons and
Accoutrements*

Albaugh, William A. *Confederate Edged Weapons*. New York: Bonanza Books, 1960.

Albaugh, W. A., Hugh Benet, Jr., and Edward Simmons. *Confederate Handguns*. Philadelphia: Riling and Lentz, 1963.

Albaugh, W. A., and William Bond. *A Photographic Supplement of Confederate Swords*. Washington, D.C.: Published privately by the authors, 1963.

Albaugh, W.A., and Edward Simmons. *Confederate Arms*. Harrisburg, Pennsylvania: Stackpole Books, 1957.

Albert, Alphaeus. *Record of American Uniform and Historical Buttons*. Boyertown, Pennsylvania: Boyertown Publications, 1977.

Berryman, Robert, ed. *The William M. Locke Collection*. East Point, Georgia: Antique Armory, n.d.

Boatner, Mark. *Civil War Dictionary*. New York: David McKay Co., 1969.

Chapel, Charles E. *Gun Collecting*. New York: Coward-McCann, 1947.

_____. *The Gun Collector's Handbook of Values*. New York: Coward-McCann, 1970.

*Much of this bibliography is from Robert M. Reilly, *United States Military Small Arms, 1816–1865*, pp. 258-59. Reprinted by perrnission.

Coggins, Jack. *Arms and Equipment of the Civil War.* New York: Doubleday and Co., 1962.

Davis, Rollin V. *U.S. Sword Bayonets, 1847–1865.* Harrisburg, Pennsylvania: Stackpole Books, 1963.

Edwards, W. B. *Civil War Guns.* Harrisburg, Pennsylvania: Stackpole Books, 1962.

Flayderman, Norman. *Guide to Antique American Firearms and Their Values.* 6th ed. New Milford, Connecticut: N. Flayderman and Co., [ordering address: P.O. Box 2446, Fort Lauderdale, Florida 33303 (305-761-8855)], 1983.

_____. *Antique Sales Catalog* (annual catalog). New Milford, Connecticut: N. Flayderman and Co., 1986.

Fuller, Claud E. *Springfield Muzzle-Loading Shoulder Arms.* New York: Francis Bannerman Sons and S and S Firearms, 1930.

_____. *The Breech Loader in the Service.* New Milford, Connecticut: N. Flayderman and Co., 1965.

_____. *The Rifled Musket.* Harrisburg, Pennsylvania: Stackpole Books, 1946.

_____. *The Whitney Firearms.* Huntington, West Virginia: Standard Publishing Co., Inc., 1946.

Fuller, Claud E., and R. D. Steuart. *Firearms of the Confederacy.* Huntington, West Virginia: Standard Publications, Inc., 1944.

Gluckman, Arcadi. *United States Martial Pistols and Revolvers.* Harrisburg, Pennsylvania: Stackpole Books, 1956.

_____. *Identifying Old United States Muskets, Rifles and Carbines.* Buffalo, New York: Otto Ulbrich Co., Inc., 1948.

Hardin, Albert N. *The American Bayonet, 1776–1964.* Philadelphia, Pennyslvania: Riling and Lentz, 1965.

Hatch, Alden. *Remington Arms in American History.* New York: Published by the author, 1961.

Haven, Charles T., and Frank A. Belden. *A History of the Colt Revolver.* New York: Bonanza Books, 1970.

Hicks, James E. *Notes on United States Ordnance: U.S. Military Firearms, 1776-1946.* LaCanada, California: Published by the author, 1962.

Karr, C. L., and C. R. Karr. *Remington Handguns.* Harrisburg, Pennsylvania: Stackpole Books, 1956.

Kirkland, Turner. *Dixie Gun Works Incorporated: Black Powder Shooting Supplies and Antique Gun Parts* (annual catalog). Union City, Tennessee: Dixie Gun Works, 1986.

Lewis, B. R. *Small Arms and Ammunition in the United States Service, 1776–1865.* Washington, D.C.: Smithsonian Institution, 1956.

Logan, Herschel C. *Cartridges.* Harrisburg, Pennsylvania: Stackpole Books, 1959.

Lord, Francis A. *Civil War Collector's Encyclopedia.* Harrisburg, Pennsylvania: Stackpole Books, 1963.

Lustyik, Andrew F. *Civil War Carbines. From Service to Sentiment.* Aledo, Illinois: Worldwide Gun Report, 1962.

Nutter, Waldo E. *Manhattan Firearms.* Harrisburg, Pennsylvania: Stackpole Books, 1958.

Parsons, John E. *Smith & Wesson Revolvers.* New York: William Morrow and Co., Inc., 1957.

_____. *The First Winchester.* New York: William Morrow and Co., Inc., 1955.

Peterson, Harold L. *Notes on Ordnance of the American Civil War, 1861–1865.* Richmond: American Ordnance Association, 1959.

_____. *The American Sword, 1775–1945.* New Hope, Pennsylvania: Robert Halter, 1954.

Rankin, Colonel Robert H. *Small Arms of the Sea Service.* New Milford, Connecticut: N. Flayderman, Inc., 1972.

Reilly, Robert M. *American Martial Flintlocks from 1775 to 1850.* Lincoln, Rhode Island: Andrew Mowbray Publishing Co., 1986.

_____. *United States Military Small Arms, 1816-1865.* Baton Rouge, Louisiana: Eagle Press, 1970.

Riling, Ray. *The Powder Flask Book.* New York: Bonanza Books, 1953.

Ripley, Warren. *Artillery and Ammunition of the Civil War.* New York: Rinehart, 1970.

Sellers, Frank. *American Gunsmiths.* Highland Park, New Jersey: Gun Room Press, 1983.

Serven, James E. *Colt Firearms, 1836–1954.* Santa Ana, California: Published by the author, 1954.

_____. *The Collecting of Guns.* Harrisburg, Pennsylvania: Stackpole Books, 1964.

Smith, Samuel, and Edward Bitters. *Historic Pistols: The American Martial Flintlock, 1760–1845.* Highland Park, New Jersey: Gun Room Press, 1985.

Wilson, R. L. *The Colt Heritage: The Official History of Colt Firearms from 1836 to the Present.* New York: Simon and Schuster, 1986.

Appendix D
A Selected Bibliography

Amann, William. *Personnel of the Civil War.* Two volumes. New York: Thomas Yoseloff, 1961.

Battles and Leaders of the Civil War. Four volumes. New York: Castle Books, 1956.

Beers, Henry P. *Guide to the Archives of the Government of the Confederate States of America.* National Archives Publication No. 68-15. Washington: General Services Administration, 1968.

Bibliography of State Participation in the Civil War. Charlottesville, Virginia: Allen Publishing Company, 1961.

Biographical Sketches of the Commissioned Officers of the Confederate States Marine Corps. (Reprint) Washington, North Carolina: Ralph W. Donnelly, 1983.

Broadfoot, Tom, Marianne Pair and Roger Hunt, eds. *Civil War Books: A Priced Checklist.* 2d ed. Wilmington, North Carolina: Broadfoot Publishing Co., 1983.

Civil War Naval Chronology. Washington, D.C.: U.S. Navy Department, 1971.

Civil War Times Illustrated. Gettysburg, Pennsylvania: Historical Times, Inc., 1962-present.

The Confederate Roll of Honor, Minutes of the Confederate Congress General Orders Number 64. Richmond, August 10, 1864. (Reprint) Mattituck, New York: J. M. Carroll and Co., 1985.

The Confederate Veteran. Vols. 1-40. Nashville, Tennessee: 1893-1932. (Reprint) Wilmington, North Carolina: Broadfoot Publishing Co., 1986.

The Confederate Veteran Magazine Index. Wilmington, North Carolina: Broadfoot Publishing Co.

Coulter, E. Merton. *Travels in the Confederate States: A Bibliography.* (Reprint) Wilmington, North Carolina: Broadfoot Publishing Co., 1981.

Cullum, George W. *Biographical Register of the Officers and Graduates of the United States Military Academy at West Point, New York, from Its Establishment, March 16, 1802, to the Reorganization of 1866-67.* New York: D. Van Nostrand, 1868.

Current, Richard, ed. *Encyclopedia of the Confederacy.* New York: Simon and Schuster, 1993.

Dictionary of American Naval Fighting Ships. Eight volumes. Washington, D.C.: Navy Department, 1959-1981.

Directory of Historical Societies and Agencies in the United States and Canada. Nashville, Tennessee: American Assn. for State and Local History, 1965.

Dornbusch, Charles E. *Military Bibliography of the Civil War.* Three volumes. New York: The New York Public Library, 1961-72.

Dyer, Frederick H. *A Compendium of the War of the Rebellion.* Des Moines, Iowa: Dyer Publishing Co., 1908. (Reprint) Three volumes. New York: Thomas Yoseloff, 1959. (Reprint) Two volumes. Dayton, Ohio: Morningside Bookshop, forthcoming.

Evans, Clement A. *Confederate Military History.* Twelve volumes. Atlanta, Georgia: Confederate Publishing Co., 1899.

Gardner, Alexander. *Gardner's Photographic Sketch Book of the Civil War.* Washington, D.C.: Philip and Solomons, 1865. (Reprint) New York: Dover Press, 1959. (Other reprints)

Guide to Genealogical Research in the National Archives. Washington, D.C.: National Archives and Records Service, 1983.

Hamer, Philip. *A Guide to Archives and Manuscripts in the United States.* New Haven: Yale University Press, 1961.

Hamersly, Thomas H. S. *Complete Regular Army Register of the United States: For 100 Years (1779–1879).* Washington: Thomas H. S. Hamersly, 1880.

Hamersly, Lewis. *The Records of Living Officers of the United States Navy and Marine Corps.* Philadelphia: J. B. Lippincott and Co., 1870.

Heitman, Francis B. *Historical Register and Dictionary of the United States Army, from Its Organization, September 29, 1789, to March 2, 1903.* Washington: Government Printing Office, 1903. (Reprint) Urbana, Illinois: University of Illinois Press, 1965.

The History of the Confederate States Marine Corps. (Reprint) Washington, North Carolina: Ralph W. Donnelly, 1976.

The Image of War: 1861–1865. Six volumes. Harrisburg, Pennsylvania: National Historical Society, 1981-1984.

Kirkham, E. Kay. *The Handwriting of American Records for a Period of 300 Years.* Logan, Utah: Everton Publishers, 1973.

A List of Field Officers, Regiments and Battalions in the Confederate States Army, 1861–1865. (Reprint) Mattituck, New York: J. M. Carroll and Co., 1983.

A List of Log Books of the United States Navy, Stations, and Miscellaneous Units, 1801-1947 (Special List 44). Washington, D.C.: National Archives and Records Service, 1986.

A List of Staff Officers of the Confederate States Army, 1861-1865. (Reprint) Mattituck, New York: J. M. Carroll and Co., 1983.

Military Operations of the Civil War: A Guide-Index to the Official Records of the Union and Confederate Armies, 1861-1865. Washington, D.C.: National Archives and Records Service, General Services Administration, U.S. Government Printing Office, 1968.

Military Service Records: A Select Catalog of National Archives Microfilm Publications. Washington, D.C.: National Archives and Records Service, 1985.

Miller, Franics T. *The Photographic History of the Civil War.* Ten volumes. New York: Review of Reviews Company, 1911. (Reprint) Five volumes. New York: Thomas Yoseloff, 1957.

Minor, Kate P. *An Author and Subject Index to the Southern Historical Society Papers,* Vols. 1-38. Richmond, Virginia: Superintendent of Public Printing, 1913. (Reprint) Dayton, Ohio: Morningside Bookshop, 1970.

Munden, Kenneth W., and Henry P. Beers. *Guide to Federal Archives Relating to the Civil War.* National Archives Publication No. 63-1. Washington: General Services Administration, 1962.

Papers of the Military Historical Society of Massachusetts. Fifteen volumes, with a new index. Wilmington, North Carolina: Broadfoot Publishing Company.

The Register of Officers of the Confederate States Navy, 1861-1865. (Reprint) Mattituck, New York: J. M. Carroll and Co., 1983.

Regulations for the Army of the Confederate States. (Reprint) Harrisburg, Pennsylvania: National Historical Society, 1980.

Revised Regulations for the United States Army. (Reprint) Harrisburg, Pennsylvania: National Historical Society, 1980.

Service Records of Confederate Enlisted Marines. (Reprint) Washington, North Carolina: Ralph W. Donnelly, 1979.

Southern Historical Society Papers. (Reprint) fifty-five volumes, with a new three-volume index. Wilmington, North Carolina: Broadfoot Publishing Company.

Symbols of American Libraries. Washington: Library of Congress, 1969.

Tancig, William. *Confederate Military Land Units.* New York: Thomas Yoseloff (A. S. Barnes), 1967.

The Union Army: A History of Military Affairs in the Loyal States, 1861-65. Eight volumes. Madison, Wisconsin: Federal Publishing Co., 1908.

Appendix E

Addresses of Civil War Sites
That Will Participate in the Civil War Soldier's System

ARKANSAS
Arkansas Post National Memorial
Rt. 1, Box 16
Gillett, Arkansa 72055

Pea Ridge National Military Park
P.O. Box 700
Pea Ridge, Arkansas 72751

DISTRICT OF COLUMBIA
Ford's Theater National Historic Site
c/o National Capitol Parks, Central
900 Ohio Drive, SW
Washington, D.C. 20242

Fredrick Douglass National Historic Site
1411 W Street SE
Washington, D.C. 20020-4813

Rock Creek Park (Fort Stevens)
5000 Glover Road, NW
Washington, D.C. 20015

FLORIDA
Fort Jefferson National Monument
c/o Everglades National Park
P.O. Box 279
Homestead, Florida 33030

Gulf Islands National Seashore (Forts Barrancas, Pickens, and Massachu-
    setts)
1801 Gulf Breeze Parkway
Gulf Breeze, Florida 32561

GEORGIA
Andersonville National Historic Site
Route 1, Box 800
Andersonville, Georgia 31711

Chickamauga and Chattanooga National Military Park
P. O. Box 2128
Fort Oglethorpe, Georgia   30742

Fort Pulaski National Monument
P.O. Box 30757
Savannah, Georgia 31410

Kennesaw Mountain National Battlefield Park
900 Kennesaw Mountain Drive
Kennesaw, Georgia 30144-4854

ILLINOIS
Lincoln Home National Historic Site
413 South Eighth Street
Springfield, Illinois   62701

INDIANA
Lincoln Boyhood National Memorial
P.O. Box 1816
Lincoln City, Indiana 47552

KANSAS
Fort Scott National Historic Site
Old Fort Boulevard
Fort Scott, Kansas 66701-1471

KENTUCKY
Abraham Lincoln Birthplace National Historic Site
2995 Lincoln Farm Road
Hodgenville, Kentucky 42748

Cumberland Gap National Historical Park
P.O. Box 1848
Middlesboro, Kentucky 40965

LOUISIANA
Jean Lafitte National Historic Park and Preserve
365 Canal Street, Suite 3080
New Orleans, Louisiana 70130

MARYLAND
Antietam National Battlefield
P.O. Box 58
Sharpsburg, Maryland 21782

Fort McHenry National Monument and Historic Shrine
East Fort Avenue
Baltimore, Maryland 21230-5393

Fort Washington Park
National Capitol Parks, East
1900 Anacostia Drive, SE
Washington, D.C. 20020

Monocacy National Battlefield
4801 Urbana Pike
Frederick, Maryland 21701

MISSISSIPPI
Brices Cross Roads National Battlefield Site
c/o Natchez Trace Parkway
R.R.1, NT-143
Tupelo, Mississippi 38801

Natchez Trace National Scenic Trail
c/o Natchez Trace Parkway
R.R. 1, NT-143
Tupelo, Mississippi 38801

Tupelo National Battlefield
c/o Natchez Trace Parkway
R.R. 1, NT-143
Tupelo, Mississippi 38801

Vicksburg National Military Park
3201 Clay Street
Vicksburg, Mississippi 39180

MISSOURI
Ulysses S. Grant National Historic Site
7400 Grant Street
St. Louis, Missouri 63123

Wilson's Creek National Battlefield
Route 2, Box 75
Republic, Missouri 65738

NEW MEXICO
Pecos National Historical Park
P.O. Drawer 418
Pecos, New Mexico 87522

NEW YORK
Grant's Tomb
c/o Manhattan Sites/NPS
26 Wall Street
New York, New York 10005

PENNSYLVANIA
Gettysburg National Military Park
P.O. Box 1080
Gettysburg, Pennsylvania 17325

SOUTH CAROLINA
Fort Sumter National Monument
1214 Middle Street
Sullivan's Island, South Carolina 29482

TENNESSEE
Andrew Johnson National Historic Site
P.O. Box 1088
Greeneville, Tennessee 37744

Shiloh National Military Park
Route 1, Box 9
Shiloh, Tennessee 38376

Stones River (Murfreesboro) National Battlefield
Murfreesboro, Tennessee 37129

(See also)
Chickamauga and Chattanooga National Military Park
Natchez Trace National Scenic Trail/Parkway

VIRGINIA
Appomattox Court House National Historical Park
P.O. Box 218
Appomattox, Virginia 24522

Arlington House
The Robert E. Lee Memorial
c/o George Washington Memorial Parkway
Turkey Run Park
McLean, Virginia 22101

Colonial National Historical Park
P.O. Box 210
Yorktown, Virginia 23690

Fredericksburg and Spotsylvania County
    Battlefields Memorial National Military Park
120 Chatham Lane
Fredericksburg, Virginia 22405

Manassas (Bull Run) National Battlefield Park
6511 Sudley Road
Manassas, Virginia 22110

Petersburg National Battlefield
P.O. Box 549
Route 36 East
Petersburg, Virginia 23804

Richmond National Battlefield Park
3215 East Broad Street
Richmond, Virginia 23223

Shenandoah National Park
Route 4, Box 348
Luray, Virginia 22835

WEST VIRGINIA
Harpers Ferry National Historical Park
P.O. Box 65
Harpers Ferry, West Virginia 25425

Index